66 The miracle of American democracy is that people with different points of view, different priorities, and different concerns can come together and collaborate in service of the common good. As Owen Paepke points out, that fundamental element of our system is now at risk. For America to prosper and succeed in the 21st century, our leaders will need to put problem-solving above politicking. *The Purple Presidency 2024* helps illuminate how we got here and provides a blueprint for a better politics."

—**NANCY JACOBSON**, FOUNDER AND
CEO OF NO LABELS

66 Many voters—particularly those in their 20s and 30s—are concerned about the 2024 election. They're not worried about voter suppression or election security. Their real fear is having to choose again between Donald Trump and Joe Biden. They're desperate for another choice. *The Purple Presidency 2024* presents a clear blueprint for an independent movement in America and a powerful argument that now is the time. I hope our country has the wisdom to follow it."

—**NEAL SIMON**, AUTHOR OF *CONTRACT TO UNITE
AMERICA* AND 2018 INDEPENDENT CANDIDATE FOR
U.S. SENATE

66 In *The Purple Presidency 2024*, Owen Paepke makes compelling arguments about why our political system is broken and what we might do to fix it. This book takes us convincingly down the path of how we got here and where we might go. I love that he urges all of us to make a difference, because we have no time to waste."

—JIM SPURLINO, AUTHOR OF
LOSING OUR ELECTIONS AND *BUSINESS BULLSEYE*

66 The dangerous drift toward extremism in both parties has brought us to a tipping point—either we remind ourselves of our common humanity and when and why our politics and democracy once worked or we continue further into the abyss. *The Purple Presidency 2024* is a clarion call for the majority of Americans who believe in good government to make their voices heard. We must show independence by no longer blindly following the two-party system."

—BOB WORSLEY, RETIRED ARIZONA STATE SENATOR,
INDEPENDENT REPUBLICAN, AND AUTHOR OF
THE HORSESHOE VIRUS

THE PURPLE PRESIDENCY 2024

Publishing

realclearpublishing.com

The Purple Presidency 2024: How Voters Can Reclaim the White House for Bipartisan Governance

For more information, please contact:
RealClear Publishing, an imprint of Amplify Publishing Group
620 Herndon Parkway, Suite 320
Herndon, VA 20170
info@amplifypublishing.com

Library of Congress Control Number: 2022923825

CPSIA Code: PRV0223A

ISBN-13: 978-1-63755-741-9

Printed in the United States

To younger generations of Americans,

in the hope that our national experiment

will never be allowed to fail.

THE PURPLE PRESIDENCY

2024

HOW VOTERS CAN RECLAIM THE WHITE
HOUSE FOR BIPARTISAN GOVERNANCE

C. OWEN PAEPKE

RealClear
Publishing

CONTENTS

INTRODUCTION

A house divided against itself cannot stand.
—Abraham Lincoln, 1858

Things fall apart, the centre cannot hold.
Mere anarchy is loosed upon the world.
The best lack all conviction,
While the worst are full of passionate intensity.
—William Butler Yeats, 1919

Nothing is written.
—Lawrence of Arabia, 1926

America deserves better presidents. Donald Trump and Joe Biden have been the most unpopular presidents since polling began. Each thoroughly earned voters' low regard by ignoring or mishandling the nation's fundamental and pressing problems. Trump became the first one-term president in three decades, and Biden may be poised to replicate that feat in 2024. Yet they remain their own biggest fans, touting imagined accomplishments, blaming their critics, and refusing to address their own shortcomings or accept responsibility for their mistakes in office.

Successful presidents rise above setbacks and course correct to minimize their faults. Presidents Ronald Reagan and Bill Clinton faced tough challenges and opposition during their first terms but won decisive reelections by working *with* their opposition to meet those challenges. Trump and Biden responded to adversity by dividing, denying, complaining, maligning critics, and doubling down on their failures, achieving very little.

Trump is seeking the Republican nomination for 2024. His fervent cadre of supporters and unique talent for sabotaging other contenders could make him the first-ever Republican presidential candidate in three consecutive elections. Biden remains the favorite among likely Democratic voters, if he runs. Most Americans reject these choices, hoping that neither will run again and wishing that Candidate NOTA (None Of The Above) were on the ballot. Each may be the only opponent the other could defeat.

A system that could even contemplate renominating such unworthy and unwanted candidates is fundamentally broken. "Dysfunctional" is too timid an adjective to describe the current state of presidential politics.

More of the same will produce more of the same. Many younger Americans have never experienced voting for a candidate they really wanted as their president. This privilege has degenerated into voting against the greater of two evils. With each such choice, corrosive cynicism works itself deeper into the nation's psyche. It threatens to become the new normal.

This short book is a plea for America to demand at least one deserving moderate or centrist presidential candidate in 2024. It appeals to the most fundamental tenets of democracy. Presidents Trump and Biden were duly nominated and elected under the auspices of political parties dating back more than a century, but most Americans do not want to be governed by either of them and probably never did. The parties themselves have taken on an undemocratic overlay, offering candidates most Americans would never choose as their president and debasing their votes on election day. These have been the parties' presidents rather than the people's. In office, they have lived down to voters' expectations. Little wonder that "discouraging words" dominate the public discourse. Negative sentiments are pervasive, and they should be.

But the sheer bleakness of this picture may present the best opportunity for changing it. *Few Americans want more of the same,* yet the major parties seem intent on delivering just that. The parties and their presidents boast of their wonderful accomplishments in power, while the

American people overwhelmingly see a nation in decline, blaming poor and divisive leadership in Washington. This disconnect between voters and their supposed representatives is stunning, but it has become business as usual, barely raising an eyebrow.

The parties will not change on their own. Most presidential aspirants now share negative favorability ratings in the polls and offer fringe policies that most voters are keen to reject. Until this century, that never happened. Candidates reflected America.

Poor leadership is hurting the nation badly. Neglected problems are becoming crises. The national debt has reached potentially dangerous levels. Feckless yo-yo policies on energy self-sufficiency and climate change have frittered away a decade that should have advanced the next energy revolution. Both parties fiddled while Social Security's finances burned. Dictators have seized the global initiative, putting the free world on the defensive. The 2024 election may be the last clear chance to reverse such trends before they spin out of control.

Meanwhile, both parties have deserted their traditional core supporters in favor of fringes that will never produce a national consensus for action; indeed, they seem to relish creating even more division. Each seems committed to nominating another radically unsuitable and broadly unpopular presidential candidate in 2024. This is political malpractice, and it defies the bedrock principle of democracy: people have the right to choose the leaders they want.

This spells opportunity for a moderate or centrist. *If the 2024 ballots include a credible presidential candidate committed to representing mainstream voters, those voters can write American political history.*

The voters do not yet embrace this vision. Faced with partisan hubris, they feel helpless, but they, and they alone, have the power to fix this broken system if they commit to that end by placing nation above party. When the major parties cannot or will not nominate candidates who represent the views of most Americans, instill pride in their nation, and take responsibility for leading this nation out of its current morass, voters need to reclaim their rights and perform their democratic duty. The 2024 election is the time for drastic action, not in media rants or on the streets or over drinks but at the ballot box, as America's founders intended.

This book is roughly divided into past, present, and future. Chapter One briefly describes the intense political polarization that has enveloped America in this century, its drivers, and its consequences. Chapter Two addresses national challenges that polarization has prevented Washington from resolving. Chapter Three sketches a picture of what moderate and centrist voters, whether Republicans, Democrats, or independents, could do to combat this rising partisanship and reverse the nation's declining prospects, if we choose to write that history.

CHAPTER ONE

THE NEED

I didn't leave the Democratic party. The party left me.
—Ronald Reagan, 1962

I didn't leave the Republican party.
The Republican party left me.
—John Kasich, 2018

C ongress has become too polarized, representing groups and ideologies lying far outside the national mainstream. Beginning with George Washington, presidents have had to resist such polarization and unify the nation by brokering compromises, moderating their own parties' extremist tendencies, and appealing to mainstream voters of both parties to produce solutions with broad support.

Recent presidents have not merely failed in curtailing excessive partisanship, they have exacerbated it, encouraging their own parties' worst tendencies by promoting extreme agendas while ridiculing or dismissing opposing views. The result has been a nation headed in the wrong direction, a conclusion already reached by clear voter majorities in both parties and an even larger majority of independents.

A Bipolar Congress

Something has gone terribly wrong when the biggest threat to our American economy is the American Congress.
—Joe Manchin, 2013

We're getting nothing done, my friends, we're getting nothing done.
—John McCain, 2017

Political scientists have an accepted measure, called DW-NOMINATE, for measuring political ideology, that is, a politician's tendency toward conservatism or liberalism. The following graph[1] shows the distribution of DW-NOM-INATE scores for the recently ended 117th Congress:

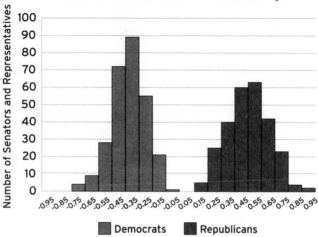

DW-NOMINATE scores for 117th Congress

Democrats and Republicans form lovely bell curves on their own, but those curves are *completely distinct*, with zero overlap, like mapping giraffes and quarter horses on the same height chart. Most voters reside in that chasm at the center. Their supposed representatives do not. Every single Democrat is more liberal than every single Republican, and moderates in either party have become endangered species. This is political and ideological bipolarity at its most extreme.

Younger Americans may assume that this condition is normal, but it is in fact unique to twenty-first-century Congresses. Compare the same chart for the Congress of 1971–72:

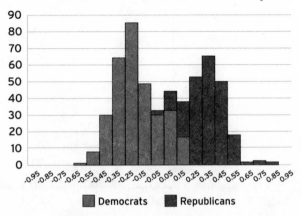

DW-NOMINATE scores for 92nd Congress

Democrats ■ Republicans

Partisan bipolarity existed then as well, but with narrower differences and considerable overlap in the center. That center comprised over one hundred Democrats and Republicans with comparable ideological profiles, with another hundred immediately adjacent on the left or right. These two hundred could usually find common ground on major and contentious measures, and their consensus wielded bipartisan strength in the Congress and with the White House.

This difference is stark. The current Congress *has no center*; statistically, centrists are the null set. Any centrist or moderate proposal begins with no natural supporters under the Capitol dome. Democrats resist it as too conservative, Republicans as too liberal. Such proposals must gain majority support in both houses starting from zero, a daunting proposition. This usually becomes a recipe for rancor and inaction, with extreme members of both parties defining their public positions.

Confirmation of Supreme Court justices highlights the emergence of this polarized Congress. Until recently, partisan opposition to reputable judicial nominees was almost unthinkable. The Senate confirmed the deeply conservative Justice Scalia 98–0 and the equally liberal Justice Ruth Bader Ginsburg 96–3. Compare the same process in 2021 and 2020, when bitter hearings laden with innuendo and blatantly political questioning preceded the confirmations of Justice Ketanji Brown Jackson by a 53–47 margin and Justice Amy Coney Barrett by 52–48. This partisan process undermines the legitimacy of the Court, making it look like an extension of political war by other means. Some Democrats threatened court-packing if Barrett were confirmed, a thinly veiled attack on the Constitution's carefully crafted separation of powers. Congress' willingness to pack the Court when needed to cement desired objectives would have effectively nullified the independence of the judiciary.

Such misuse of the confirmation authority for partisan purposes knows no inherent bounds or legal restrictions. A Republican-majority Senate might refuse to confirm *every* nominee by a Democratic president, or vice versa. Extended to cabinet nominations, this could bring a new administration to a standstill before it even began.

The legislative record of 2021 illustrates the rise of partisan gridlock. Despite control of the White House, the House, and the Senate (counting the vice president's tie-breaking vote), Democrats enacted only one worthwhile bill in President Biden's first year. The Bipartisan Infrastructure Bill originated as part of a $6 trillion spending bill crafted by Senator Bernie Sanders, which was stuffed with new government programs in keeping with his socialist beliefs. Republicans voiced support for physical infrastructure investments while opposing the broader social and policy scope of the original bill. This narrower and much less expensive bill passed the Senate with a solid bipartisan majority and commanded comfortable majority support in the House. Nevertheless, the Progressive Caucus stalled it for months in the House, with Biden's encouragement, holding it hostage to coerce Senate passage of the "social infrastructure" programs in Build Back Better (BBB). When nine moderate House Democrats called this bluff by threatening to side with Republicans, the party's liberal wing was outraged, treating a principled stand supporting bipartisan compromise as a betrayal of all that was holy. After weeks of backbiting, this stonewalling finally crumbled, and the measure passed easily. This was constructive legislation, albeit with unnecessary partisan drama in the process.

Despite the nation's glaring challenges in 2021, domestic and foreign, economic, social, and even medical, Congress passed nothing else of any lasting benefit. It spent most of its time flogging BBB, a progressive Democratic wish list that was doomed in the Senate from inception. This paralleled President Trump's first year in office as Republican majorities in both House and Senate occupied their time trying to repeal the Affordable Care Act and accomplished little else.

Compare these records to that of the 104th Congress (with a Democratic president and a Republican Speaker), which passed comprehensive welfare reform, HIPAA, an overhaul of the telecommunications law, and immigration reform, among other bills, all while beginning the process of balancing the budget. Or to the 99th Congress (Republican president, Democratic Speaker), which passed sweeping overhauls of federal budgeting, the tax code, and the Department of Defense, along with outlawing age discrimination. Congress worked while bipartisanship still held sway.

Negotiation and compromise between the parties yield durable solutions, while purely partisan efforts produce gridlock and too little else. The "do-nothing" epithet coined by President Truman now describes business as usual in the Capitol, the sorry result of twenty-first-century polarization.

Partisans in Chief

Every election is determined by the people who show up.
—Professor Larry Sabato, 2020

As Congress became ever more polarized, the ship of state needed a stabilizing, centering presence in the White House to maintain an even keel. It has gotten the opposite, thanks to the broken nomination process and a toxic political environment.

Over the past several decades, America's major parties have adopted "a nomination system unlike that of any other major democracy in the world."[2] That uniqueness has been a vice, not a virtue. Scholarly books have been written about the resulting problems. For current purposes, a few paragraphs will serve.

Party leaders formerly selected presidential nominees in notorious "smoke-filled rooms." Presidential primaries were few and relatively unimportant. They were "arenas in which candidates could showcase their qualities or demonstrate their electability,"[3] in effect, beauty pageants—nonbinding devices for party leaders to observe major contenders on the stump. As recently as 1968, Vice President Hubert Humphrey became the Democratic nominee without winning any primaries. This nominating process was undemocratic, as intended. Parties chose candidates; democracy got its turn in the general election.

In this century, however, American voters have picked the candidates, making presidential primaries much like House primaries on a larger stage. This sounded good to reformers but has backfired in practice. Paradoxically, more democracy became undemocratic by emboldening candidates with intense fringe followings—in a crowded field, the united few usually defeat the divided many. Even unimpressive pluralities play out as victories.

Moreover, *primary voters tend to be louder, angrier, and more extreme than mainstream Americans*. Statistically, they are left of most Democrats or right of most Republicans in their views—in a word, fringy— enhancing the prospects of the most polarized candidates at the expense of moderates commanding broader but less intense support. Registered independents widely outnumber either Democrats or Republicans, and they tend to inhabit the center of the policy spectrum. They rarely vote in party primaries, for reasons explained in Chapter Two.

Primary results do not reflect America's preferences. Activists numbering in the tens or perhaps hundreds of thousands in each party are dictating general election choices for 150 million Americans.

The rise of the web and other digital media was

supposed to provide more diverse information sources, producing a better-informed electorate. In practice, it helped to destabilize the political environment and exacerbate this primary-based polarization. Most traditional media followed certain conventions, where journalists actually gathered information and verified facts before publication. The new media outlets mostly scorn any such standards or safeguards.[4] Partisan bloggers are political entrepreneurs who thrive on creating rage. They routinely post whatever might help their causes, with little regard for facts or fairness. The web makes these unequal sources appear equally reliable. Too many readers or listeners, unable or unwilling to distinguish between journalistic reporting and bloviating, succumb to a radical skepticism, treating all sources as reliable or suspect based on their preexisting biases. Truth and falsehood often seem like quaint artifacts of more innocent times; the only test is effectiveness in reaching a desired end, whatever the merits of an issue. John Milton's assertion that truth will prevail in the marketplace of ideas rarely finds confirmation in the blogosphere.

This proliferation of unreliable sources promotes and legitimizes the alternative realities cherished by the fringes. The rising popularity of these unfiltered outlets even tempted formerly reputable news organizations into becoming wholly owned subsidiaries of the major parties or, worse, the fringe elements of those parties. The nightly lineup of Fox News features five hours of relentlessly right-wing commentary, with no leavening and little indication of adult supervision. MSNBC begins the day with *Morning Joe* and ends it with Rachel Maddow. These are a far cry from Chet Huntley and David Brinkley or Walter Cronkite. Instead of reporting news, they blend fact, conjecture, and ideology to reach predetermined, highly partisan conclusions.

The overarching message of these partisan medias is sometimes explicit and always clear enough: the opposing party's agenda will, if unchecked, destroy the nation as we know it. Millions of Americans on both sides embrace this apocalyptic proposition. Rising extremism fostered by these media partisans reached a tipping point in the already skewed primary electorates, where the fringes have seized working control of both parties. Political doomsday prophecies could become self-fulfilling if too many voters believe them.

A nominating process that anoints small and unrep-resentative factions, granting them decisive control over voters' choice of candidates, has created a tyranny of the minority. Primary polarization turns presidential campaigns into nastier, more partisan affairs, yielding nominees with little regard for their opponents, majority rule, or compromise as an essential tool of governance. The loser then refuses to recognize the victor's legitimacy. Name-calling substitutes for rational discourse. And the wrong person resides in the White House, again.

The 2016 and 2020 presidential elections did not invent these tendencies, but they certainly intensified them.

With no incumbent in the 2016 race, both parties experienced the full force of primary-centric elections. Hillary Clinton began as the prohibitive favorite Democrat. No one dared enter the lists against the Clinton machine except a septuagenarian democratic socialist from a tiny state with little name recognition, limited funding, a meager legislative record in the Senate, and a stump speech that ran the full gamut from anger to fury. As a Hollywood script, this would have failed the plausibility test. By any traditional standards, Senator Sanders fell well short of presidential material. Seasoned political advisers from the Clinton administration secretly welcomed him as an easy opponent to vanquish, offering their candidate a risk-free opportunity to tune up her campaign through a few early primaries, until Sanders bowed to the inevitable and went home to fulminate in Vermont.

Those advisers failed to realize how much had

changed. Sanders caught fire, drawing larger and more enthusiastic crowds than Clinton and achieving very competitive primary results until shortly before the convention. The explanation is obvious, yet rarely acknowledged. *Sanders' views, though fringy for America as a whole, lie at the heart of the liberal minority of the liberal minority that dominates the Democrats' primary electorate. Any Democrat aligned with those positions has an excellent chance of winning the nomination.* It mattered little that "his plans for governing were delusional."[5] Primaries cultivate the extreme environments where such candidates prosper.

The success and staying power of the Sanders campaign drew Clinton far to the left, where she stayed for the general election. This separated her from Clinton administration policies that retained mainstream appeal. While President Clinton had famously declared that "the era of big government is over," Hillary Clinton promised to double down on the Obama administration's government expansions. She committed to widen Social Security and Medicare eligibility and increase benefits (despite rapidly dwindling trust funds), end oil and gas exploration on federal lands, reduce prison sentences, and fight for a $15 federal minimum wage (equivalent to $17.55 in 2022), which would have represented a middle-class income in lower cost of living states. While President Clinton had coexisted constructively with Speaker Newt Gingrich and charmed many Republicans, Hillary Clinton offhand-edly consigned half of Trump's supporters to a "basket of deplorables," millions of American citizens who were beyond redemption and beneath her contempt. This tends to discourage dialogue.

Clinton had abandoned her "New Democrat" stance. This damaged her brand among moderate supporters, reducing their turnout, and even turned some work-ing-class Reagan Democrats to Trump in the critical "Blue Wall" states, a high price to pay for placating the Sanders voters who had opposed her. It surely energized and recommitted Republicans who were deeply ambiv-alent about their candidate but feared this Clinton 2.0 avatar even more.

Meanwhile, after eight years of the Obama adminis-tration, Tea Party Republicans and their offshoots were mad as hell and not going to take it anymore. On cue, Donald Trump channeled their rage, filling the Bernie Sanders role for right-wing voters with even more primary success. Few initially took his candidacy seriously, probably including Trump himself. He had no political experience or organization. He bragged about molesting women. His verbal gaffes, flip-flops, and falsehoods were enough to sink ten candidates. Many of his past policy stances had been anathema to mainstream Republicanism. Former Republican presidents, presidential candidates, senators, and respected conservative commentators shunned him. As he gained traction, a Republican NeverTrump movement coalesced behind Ohio governor John Kasich.

None of which mattered. Right-wingers had tired of moderation and negotiation. Another respected mainstream candidate in the mold of John McCain or Mitt Romney would be weak tea when a stronger brew was needed. They wanted someone who shared their anger, who defied proprieties, rules, and received wisdom of all persuasions, and who would bully his way through and drain the swamp—who would be, in short, an autocrat in word and deed. Their passion carried them to the primary polling booths while most traditional Republicans, whether undecided or unimpressed with the herd of traditional candidates, stayed home. Trump's fringe supporters may have represented a minority even among primary voters—he generally polled in the thirties in the early contests—but the remaining votes were spread among a dozen other candidates. Before the altered reality of the primaries sank in, he was unstoppable.

Smoke-filled rooms look better and better when compared to this partisan overreach of direct democracy. *If the major parties cannot or will not nominate candidates who represent the views and values of most Americans, what purpose do they serve?* Something needs to change.

The general election brought a different electorate to bear, including many more independent voters and moderate party members. Primary results did not reflect these voters' preferences. Quite the contrary—the primaries had delivered the least popular pair of candidates in post-WWII history (a record soon to be broken). But the damage had been done. America was doomed to an unsuitable president; the only question was which one.

Both candidates ran caustically negative campaigns. Neither of them offered platforms that appealed to most mainstream voters, or even tried. This left many Americans with no one to support. Instead, most cast their votes against the greater of two evils. In polling shortly preelection, half of all voters described their choice as "primarily a vote against" the opponent.[6] (Such "nega-votes" accounted for about one-third of the total in the 2008 McCain-Barack Obama race, still too high, but much lower than in 2016.) Clinton, the better-known figure with a lengthy public record, had accumulated more nega-votes during her career, enough to flip the race in Trump's favor in an epic upset.

Trumpocracy

Trump completely misconstrued his least-bad-option victory, preferring to believe that his adoring rally crowds had placed him in the White House with a mission. He governed according to his and his loyalists' wishes, systematically adding to his nega-vote ledger and predictably leading to his 2020 defeat.

Trump maintained only a tenuous and adversarial relationship with any reality that conflicted with his beliefs and pretensions. Announcing his candidacy, he had declared that "I will build a great great wall on our southern border, and I'll have Mexico pay for that wall." Most of the wall was never built, and Mexico paid nothing, but Trump later declared success, claiming he meant instead that the trade deal he struck, which did not exist when he made the claim, would repay the cost of the wall.

He reflexively responded to any opposition with ridicule, and his capacity for offending others knew no boundaries and counted no costs. He belittled Senator John McCain's heroic war record. He called Germany's chancellor Angela Merkel "stupid" and British prime minister Theresa May "a fool." He had a public spat with French president Emmanuel Macron. Insulting key allies was a novel approach for the leader of the free world.

The only national rulers seemingly immune from his invective were autocrats. He displayed mostly admiration for Russian president Vladimir Putin and Chinese president Xi Jinping, who were systematically undermining America's interests around the globe, and praised North Korean dictator Kim Jong-Un as "a great leader."

Domestically, Trump showered his political allies and appointees with praise, until they dared to disagree with him, when he would revert to his *Apprentice* persona. The carnage among senior staff was gruesome, and their memoirs were brutal. The victim of his most extreme and unjust reversal was Vice President Mike Pence, who served Trump loyally through four years of embarrassments but refused to reject the states' duly certified counts of electors on January 6 to delay Biden's inevitable inauguration. Pence was instantly dead to Trump and remains so today.

Trump's approval rating descended into the forties after his election and stayed there. The 2018 midterms repudiated Trump and the party that supported him. Democrats gained forty-one seats, with a popular-vote margin of +8.6 percent, compared to +5.7 percent for Republicans in the 2014 midterms. Trump had turned the American public against his party. Republicans lost the most ground among independents, who had hoped in vain for a more inclusive administration.

Trump's unpopularity mystified him—after all, his rally crowds still loved him. By dismissing adverse polls as "fake," he forfeited his chance to learn from them, sealing his own demise.

Over his four years in office, Trump became the most unpopular president since such polling began. His inconsistent and sometimes bizarre reaction to the pandemic mostly cemented existing negative impressions. He retained the support of his partisans but alienated most mainstream voters.

Trump hit new lows following his refusal to accept his election loss or to provide actual evidence supporting his fraud claims in even one of over sixty lawsuits challenging the results. His lawyers presented only accusations, some refuted, some simply fantastic, positing elaborate secret conspiracies involving thousands of people dedicated to undermining his flawless leadership and stealing the White House from its rightful owner. Judges, including Trump appointees, dismissed every suit, often with harsh opinions deploring their lack of any basis in fact.[7] Some of his attorneys faced judicial sanctions or ethics charges for pursuing frivolous claims or misrepresenting the record, a cardinal sin in this kind of accelerated proceeding. This zero percent success rate in court never fazed Trump's rhetoric; it became another inconvenient reality to ignore.

America dislikes a sore loser, but this offense goes deeper. In Trump's breast beat the heart of an autocrat. Election laws and oaths of office be damned; he belonged in charge, and Biden didn't. If the tally showed him eleven thousand votes behind, Republican state officials should "find" twelve thousand more Trump votes. In the final weeks preceding President Biden's inauguration, Trump continued insisting to his White House staff that he would remain in office, as if he had some say over the matter.

Smooth and peaceful transitions of power to election opponents are the defining hallmark of representative democracies, a form of governance that the founding fathers practically invented. To assure impartiality, elections must be conducted using well-defined processes; they are not freelance or subjective explorations. Designated state officials count and recount the votes if necessary to decide who won their elections, subject to judicial review for election fraud. A sitting president can have no role in that process, as an obvious matter of fairness to the challenger, who lacks the president's power to meddle. The process has fixed time frames to assure a timely handover of authority. It is un-American to continue denying election results certified by the proper authorities and upheld by the courts. When that procedure is complete, so is the election; a candidate's opinions as to what *really must have* happened have no place. The election is over. There are no mulligans. The loser congratulates the winner, and the nation moves on.

In refusing to accept the outcomes in six states after all the processes established or allowed by law, Trump behaved like a petulant third world dictator, not an American president. He compounded this mortal sin against democracy by persuading millions of voters to distrust the election system going forward.

Not Trump

The 2020 Democratic primaries began with little change from 2016. Sanders ran from the far left, with "the Squad's"[8] endorsement. He dominated early, winning in New Hampshire and Nevada and roughly tying at the top of the Iowa caucus. Senator Elizabeth Warren, with her plans for regulating everything into submission, was also running strongly. Vice President Biden stood a distant fourth and appeared to be floundering.

This was unfolding as Democratic strategists' worst nightmare. They held the winning hand in the general election. An NBC poll showed an astonishing 46 percent of registered voters *had already decided* to vote against

Trump, whomever the Democrats nominated.[9] The election was nearly over before it began; a ham sandwich would defeat Trump. Nominating a left-wing extremist like Sanders was the only way Democrats could lose. Biden offered a plausible lifeboat.

South Carolina held the last primary before Super Tuesday. The most influential politician in that state was House Majority Whip James Clyburn, a longtime Biden friend. After he went public with his support days before the primary, South Carolina broke heavily for Biden. Prominent Democrats gratefully leaped onto this one-primary bandwagon, urging voters to unite behind Biden rather than risk prolonging an internecine struggle. This preemptive strategy worked. Biden won nine of the following week's Super Tuesday primaries, and the nomination was effectively his.

Biden's primary election campaign, such as it was, had emphasized his moderate credentials from the Senate years. He declined to endorse the far left's dreams of Medicare for all, free college education, forgiveness of student debt, wealth taxes, an open border, and defunding the police. He proposed no vast spending bills.

But with the nomination safely in hand, a leftward shift began. On July 8, joint Biden-Sanders task forces, with far-left Representatives Alexandria Ocasio-Cortez

(AOC) and Pramila Jayapal among the cochairs, released 110 pages of recommendations.[10] Sanders exulted: "the goals of the task force were to move the Biden campaign into *as progressive a direction as possible*, and I think we did that." He was correct. Like Clinton in 2016, Biden had slid sharply to the left of his own political history, and of course the country, while Sanders, with nothing to lose, scarcely budged. Sanders' views had never commanded much mainstream support, but Biden needed only his base and Trump's nega-votes to win. He and his advisers valued *party unity* over *national unity*. Candidate Biden was now on record supporting a left-wing agenda. Seven months later, President Biden, the only declared moderate in the race, sat in the Oval Office executing the only declared socialist's program.

Even more than in 2016, the progressive minority had substantively prevailed in the Democratic primaries by dragging a more moderate candidate far left in order to secure the nomination. This midcampaign lurch leftward probably reduced the number of pro-Biden votes in the general election, but this scarcely mattered—the plan was always to win with the anti-Trump votes.

The 2020 general election became the ultimate nega-vote contest. The best argument for Trump was "Biden," and the best argument for Biden was "Trump"—both compelling positions for many Americans. Trump's campaign tried to follow its 2016 formula: big rallies whipping up thousands of enthusiastic supporters with fire-breathing rhetoric. In stark contrast, Biden rarely left his basement. His was a muted and at times nearly nonexistent campaign. It was also winning, comfortably winning, as it turned out.

Trump's nega-votes did the heavy lifting. One month before the election, 63 percent of Biden's supporters said "their choice is more a vote against Trump" than for Biden,[11] eclipsing 2016's record for nega-vote dominance by a wide margin. Trump's vigorous and often strident campaign only reinforced the negative views of the not-Trump voters, strengthening their commitment to vote against him rather than just staying home. Biden's comparative silence added few if any nega-votes and may have persuaded some voters that he was the steadier pair of hands. This was arguably an ignoble strategy, but effective in the era of nega-voting dominance, providing nothing for the electorate to vote against. Trump lost the states that Biden needed, with a few more for good measure.

Biden thus won the nomination by being not-Bernie and the presidency by being not-Trump. All perfectly lawful, but such a nega-lection hardly showcases democracy. The President's powers derive "from the consent of the governed." If the voters consented to anything in 2020, it was only under duress because the major parties had given them no choice.

The Etch A Sketch Presidency

The alternate domination of one faction over another,
sharpened by the spirit of revenge, . . . is itself
a frightful despotism.
—George Washington, 1796

Though overshadowed by intellects like Thomas Jefferson, Alexander Hamilton, and Ben Franklin, President Washington proved to be remarkably prescient. Opposition politicians excluded from governance use their spare time throwing rocks and sharpening knives, preparing to indulge "the spirit of revenge" when their power returns. Polarization is not a one-off event. Like violence, it is a cycle that gains destructive power with each swing of the pendulum. The twenty-first century has displayed this cycle all too well.

President Biden governed as a left-wing Democrat from his first day in the Oval Office.[12] Examples include the following:

- **Debt and deficits:** President Biden backed new spending bills exceeding $6 trillion. Having opposed Sanders' economic agenda in the primaries, Biden adopted it in the Oval Office. "How big can we go?" became his favorite question to staffers. Would Biden ever have won that office campaigning on that question?

- **Government expansion:** President Biden's social-infrastructure spending bill proposed a Progressive Caucus wish list of new "soft" entitlements that would have permanently expanded the role of the federal government into social welfare realms traditionally governed by the states.

- **Federalized elections:** President Biden vigorously supported a federal takeover of election law to achieve registration and voter validation changes sought by Democratic candidates in some states. The states have run elections since the nation began.

- **Senate rules:** President Biden backed practical elimination of the filibuster to enable Democrats to push bills through the evenly divided Senate. Senator Biden participated in filibusters; Vice President Biden supported Democrats' filibusters in the Republican-controlled Senate; and candidate Biden never hinted at such a change of heart.

- **Afghanistan:** President Biden pulled troops out of Afghanistan before securing repatriation of civilian workers and Afghan allies, then described the result as "an extraordinary success." Those who lived through the chaos and bloodshed disagreed.

- **Civility:** Candidate Biden promised a return to civility in Washington after four years of Trump's insults. President Biden then branded opponents of Democrats' federal-elections bill as racists by equating them with George Wallace and Bull Connor. As the midterms approached, Biden labeled MAGA supporters "semifascist," while refusing to criticize Democrats for cynically promoting MAGA candidates in the midterm primaries. (See "Election Reform" in Chapter Two.) The administration's tone became ever more strident as Biden's poll numbers swooned.

- **Climate change and energy:** Beginning on his first day in office, Biden unilaterally suspended new federal oil and gas leasing, canceled pipeline projects, and broadly supported the Green lobby's campaign against all fossil fuels. Domestic producers heard the new president's message and hunkered down, deciding not to invest their stockholders' capital in new exploration and drilling in this hostile environment. Then, as energy prices soared, Biden blasted Exxon for drilling too little, denying out of hand that his policies had contributed to the supply shortage.

- **Inflation:** Biden also dismissed any notion that his trillion-dollar spending increases had triggered the broader inflationary surge, calling it "bizarre," even as leading Democratic economists acknowledged the connection and urged restraint, as described in Chapter Two.

- **Bipartisanship:** Candidate Biden promised a return to bipartisanship and cooperation in Washington. The first test of this pledge was the $1.9 trillion Bernie-Biden economic stimulus bill. Ten Republican senators approached the administration offering to negotiate a smaller stimulus. President Biden rejected that overture without discussion and approved pushing the bill through on a straight party line vote in a matter of days, because a bipartisan approach would have required time and compromise.[13] (Imagine!) That tone persisted throughout the first two years. There is no record of any substantive discussions between President Biden and his longtime Senate colleague Mitch McConnell on any topic before the midterm elections.

Many Biden voters may have expected a moderate and civil Democrat in office. Instead, they got a Bernie Sanders act-alike, a polarizing, angry administration that brooked no impertinence from Republicans and reveled in excluding them from congressional participation. Biden's popularity steadily waned as this in-office identity unfolded, with the largest deterioration among independent voters. As of October 2022, only 19 percent of independents considered the country to be on the right track,[14] with Biden shouldering most of the blame.

The 2022 Midterm Elections

A plague on both your houses.
—William Shakespeare, 1597

The White House was not at stake in 2022, but Trump and Biden were still on the ballot. Both lost.

Biden's unpopularity and dismal record in office made him the principal target of most Republican candidates. Incumbent congressional Democrats were constantly under attack for voting with Biden. He made several bizarre claims on the stump ("our economy is strong as hell"; he had cut the debt and deficit; gas prices fell during his administration), providing more fodder for his critics, as if inflation, a looming recession, the border mess, and rising crime were not strong enough headwinds. Campaigning Democrats invited Biden to keep far, far away. Among independent voters, Democrats lost five points of their edge from the 2020 election.[15] Republican House candidates received nearly 52 percent of all votes cast, compared to 46 percent in 2018, just enough to gain control.

Republicans fielded a weak slate of Senate candidates nationally, as Senator McConnell immediately recognized. Trump endorsed political novices and outliers—without experience, political followings, or funding sources—based on their fealty to Trump and his "Stop the Steal" credo. They won narrow victories in Republican primaries, but the November electorate presented an entirely different environment. Most independents reject "Stop the Steal," and Trump's involvement in the midterm just mobilized the Democrats' base to vote against his proxies and induced some Republican voters to stay home rather than support his candidate. These substandard and off-message candidates probably delivered Democratic Senate wins in Pennsylvania, Nevada, Arizona, and possibly New Hampshire easily enough to have given Republicans control.[16]

Georgia's elections may have been the most telling. Trump vigorously opposed Governor Brian Kemp's bid for reelection while backing Herschel Walker's campaign for the Senate. The same voters on the same day delivered a comfortable victory to Kemp with 2.1 million votes while Walker barely made it into a runoff with 1.9 million, a difference of 200,000 votes. The one consistent trend, in Georgia and nationwide, was rejection of Trump's preferences.

One week after the midterms, Trump declared his presidential candidacy in a triumphal gala at Mar-a-Lago. This speech showcased Trump's remarkable ability to substitute fantasy for reality. He never filled the petroleum reserve; it was full when he took office. He claimed that "no president had ever sought or received one dollar for our country from China until I came along." China's custom duties averaged $12 billion annually during the Obama administration. He trivialized climate change concerns: "They say the oceans will rise one-eighth of an inch over the next 200 to 300 years." The National Oceanic and Atmospheric Administration estimates the rise at ten inches over the next thirty years, continuing thereafter as long as the planet gets warmer.

Acknowledging that "the Republican party should have done better" in the midterms, Trump blamed the public. "The citizens . . . have not yet realized the full extent and the gravity of the pain our nation is going through." Fewer than one-third of Americans believed the nation was on the right track in October 2022, and just over one-quarter believed the economy was on the right track. They feel the pain much more keenly than Trump. Voters know how badly the nation has been governed, but they view Trump as part of the problem and certainly not part of any solution.

Weeks later, Trump validated voters' negative view in resounding fashion, writing in a statement, "Do you throw the Presidential Election Results of 2020 OUT and declare the RIGHTFUL WINNER, or do you have a NEW ELECTION?" The Constitution allows neither result, as Trump apparently realized. He continued: "A Massive Fraud of this type and magnitude allows for the termination of all rules, regulations, and articles, even those found in the Constitution."

A "massive fraud" (never proven) would not have suspended the law, much less the Constitution. Elections are final when the results are declared. A sitting president shown to have masterminded a fraudulent election victory would be impeached and convicted, and the vice president would ascend to the Oval Office. There is no "termination," no declaring the "rightful winner," and no "new election." Simply follow the Constitution. Presidents need to know such things.

Republicans' midterm weakness began and ended with Trump. Democrats' weakness began and ended with Biden. Post-election polling shows that most Americans grasp the nation's core political problem, whatever their leanings.[17] Clear majorities want neither Trump nor Biden to run again in 2024. Among prominent figures, Biden and Trump are viewed very unfavorably, along with Hillary Clinton (the other presidential candidate of the last eight years), Vice President Kamala Harris, House Speaker Nancy Pelosi, and Senators McConnell and Chuck Schumer, comprising the rest of the parties' leadership in Washington when the poll was taken. Of the various factors viewed as "hurting our democratic process," voters consider MAGA Republicans and left-wing congressional representatives the worst by a wide margin.

The problem is not defined by whether Democrats or Republicans are in charge. The problem is that both parties' leaderships have lost the bubble; they are failing the nation while leaving mainstream Americans behind.

Still, the lesser-of-two-evils mentality continues to dominate public discourse more than two years after Biden's victory. Democrats who acknowledged his many shortcomings clung to their "not as bad as Trump" mantra. Many Republicans, however incensed by the January 6 riot and Trump's denial of fundamental democratic principles, fell back on "he would still have been better than Biden." Whatever their merits, can either of those propositions justify presenting voters with such a Hobson's choice for a third consecutive presidential election? Or should the nation admit its past mistakes and undertake the measures needed to prevent their recurrence?

The United States is suffering through a "democratic recession," if not depression. The genius of American democracy is fading. Partisans and extremists have repudiated the nation's raison d'être. Government of, by, and for the people has become government of, by, and for the parties, which have done nothing to earn this newly exalted status.

Presidents of the Divided States

In every defeat are found the seeds of victory.
—Walter Mondale, 1984

Presidents Trump and Biden are easy targets, with their nearly unbroken records of poor judgment, lack of candor, detachment from reality, divisiveness, and ineffective governance in the White House, as confirmed by events and by their sustained unpopularity in the polls. But the political problems they exemplify transcend these flawed individuals and will persist after they leave the scene unless the parties reform themselves or voters decide to "take arms against this sea of troubles."

Twenty-first century presidential elections have taken on a distinctive and unhealthy pattern that departs markedly from their history. The 2000 hanging-chads contest between Vice President Al Gore and Governor George W. Bush established this new standard, with a few hundred votes in Florida deciding the election.

The Twenty-First Century Presidential Election Map[18]

George W. Bush: 271   Al Gore: 266   Toss Up: 0

This map has stayed much the same throughout this century: forty-five states (including DC) have consistently voted for the same party in at least five of the last six presidential elections. The six exceptions are Florida, Ohio, Iowa, Virginia, Colorado, and Nevada. The remaining states have been nearly foregone conclusions. One party took them for granted; the other conceded them. "Every vote matters" has become a feel-good adage that lacks real-world relevance. Campaign strategists waste neither time nor money running up their candidate's vote tallies in states that are not in play; those extra votes matter little, if at all, to the pros charged with producing them.

These are trench warfare campaigns designed to gain just enough traction on a few fronts to reach a bare majority in the Electoral College. *Nothing resembling a national election contest has occurred in this century, and campaign managers are already girding for another game of inches in 2024.*

'Twas never thus in the past. Most presidents won their elections *nationally*, not by eking out paper-thin margins in a few battleground states. Dwight Eisenhower won thirty-nine and forty-one states (out of forty-eight) in his two victories, losing only the Deep South. Lyndon Johnson won forty-five. Richard Nixon won thirty-two to Hubert Humphrey's fourteen (with Alabama governor

George Wallace carrying the Deep South) in 1968 and forty-nine in 1972. Reagan won forty-five and forty-nine states in his back-to-back landslides. George H. W. Bush won forty in 1988. Clinton, despite the midterm Republican sweep in 1994, still captured thirty-two states and 20 percent more votes than Bob Dole in 1996.

This norm set candidates' goals and campaign strategies. They wasted neither time nor energy on flipping Florida—they were out to win the support of a nation. This dictated themes with broad appeal, not the wedge issues that now prevail. Occasional extremist candidates like Barry Goldwater and George McGovern went down in flames.

Polarization reverses these expectations. Neither George W. Bush nor Barack Obama nor Donald Trump nor Joe Biden had enough mainstream appeal or a popular enough campaign platform to convert into a legislative agenda that would carry a nation. ("Compassionate conservatism" and "Hope and Change" and "Make America Great Again" do not qualify.) None of them even tried to secure a broad national mandate, either in the campaigns or in office. Each appealed to his base and enough leaning independents to win the election, however narrowly. Their margins of victory never commanded opponents' cooperation once they took office. Incrementalist campaign strategies prevailed. Beginning with Karl Rove's "base strategy" in Bush's 2004 campaign, candidates have focused on preaching to the choir, turning out every one of their existing supporters and winning a few battleground states to eke out 271 Electoral College votes. Eight years later, President Obama's reelection campaign executed Rove's strategy to perfection, winning with about half his 2008 margin of victory, but winning nonetheless.

Such base-based victories tend to be careful, sterile, and nearly issue-free affairs. Broadening the candidates' appeal by trying to persuade opposing-party voters is viewed as too risky: bipartisan appeals often offend the purest partisans by suggesting the possibility of compromise. But *election wins with no opposing party support may have little meaning when it comes to the hard work of governance.*

The 2020 election may prove to have been the base strategy's swan song. Trump's base surely turned out. He tallied seventy-four million votes compared to his sixty-three million in 2016. Although many of these were nega-Biden votes, Trump's supporters clearly voted, but his committed detractors easily overcame his pro-Trump base. With independent voters now outnumbering either party by a wide margin, the base is no longer large enough to win, while the partisanship of the base strategy energizes enough opposition to lose. That strategy no longer seems viable.

Over 158 million votes were cast in 2020. It took dedicated and passionate nega-voting on both sides to produce this record-smashing turnout. It was an ironic indictment of American democracy, barely acknowledged at the time or since. Bad candidates energized the electorate far more effectively than good candidates ever had.

Nega-vote elections are even worse than base-strategy elections in enabling the winner to govern. "Not-Clinton" and "not-Trump" majorities delivered neither mandates nor platforms for governance. They neither foreclosed nor supported any actionable initiatives while unduly alienating supporters of the loser. The winners entered office with scant support and few tools at their disposal.

When twentieth-century presidents won elections, they also won the nation. Landslides need no spin or morning-after demographic analyses by the talking heads, and no protestors carry "NOT MY PRESIDENT" placards in the streets. The victor wins a mandate to govern rather than to posture. Presidents Eisenhower, Johnson, Reagan, and Clinton did more than campaign effectively; they also *governed* effectively because they had earned the right to speak for all America on election day.

The losing party also benefits. It must accept the popular judgment and conform better to the voting majority's views or endure a long stretch in the wilderness. Witness Bill Clinton's New Democrat victory in 1992 following three consecutive Republican victories against more traditional Democratic candidates. Narrow losses have had exactly the opposite effect. They encourage doubling down on existing positions, vows to try harder, tweaks in technique, more sophisticated polling, an improved ground game, or better messaging, all in hopes of tipping the balance, however slightly. (We were *so close*; we can't quit now.) Worst of all, they encourage refinement and amplification of the negative campaign techniques designed to sow voter distrust of the opposing party.

These do nothing for better governance. Instead, they preserve the sway of extremists: until voters repudiate them, why shouldn't they remain in charge? Election results have rewarded rather than punishing excessive partisanship over the last two decades, with predictable effect. Republicans moved farther right and Democrats farther left. America has learned the wrong lessons and suffered increasingly severe consequences. A moderate candidate's success in a presidential election is the only dependable cure for this condition.

This lengthy spate of partisan rancor and ineffective governance makes it easy to forget how successful the United States has been compared to other nations. Private sector institutions and individuals deserve most of the credit. Generation after generation, science and technology delivered transformative advances in agriculture, manufacturing, transportation, communication, housing, information technology, and medicine. Capitalists and entrepreneurs expanded markets and scaled up production. Workers flocked here from around the world, finding opportunity, pushing out frontiers, and redefining their own, their families', and their new nation's futures.

Government played its role at critical junctures. Jefferson cemented the nation's geographic destiny. Abraham Lincoln reunited it and began purging the original sin of slavery. Franklin Roosevelt saw it through the Great Depression and defeated evil dictators in World War II. The states instituted universal K–12 education and public colleges. Twentieth-century presidents built out or facilitated power grids, interstate highways, airports, and other critical infrastructure to knit the sprawling nation together.

The tangible evidence of this success is everywhere. Each generation of Americans has lived longer, richer, and more diverse lives than their parents, until now. Millennials can hardly imagine, much less expect, such rosy futures. Most consider it unlikely that their standard of living will ever rise to their parents' level.[19] Hard data support their skepticism and their growing discontent. Life expectancies are shortening, not lengthening. Twenty-somethings struggle financially, own less, and depend more on their parents than in any recent generation. America's long legacy of progress has been interrupted, and its future is uncertain at best.

Polarized and inept twenty-first century governance deserves much of the blame, becoming the single greatest threat to the nation's identity. Without prompt and decisive action at the top, that legacy will slip into history.

This chapter has painted a grim and disturbing picture. Though accurate, it is more a snapshot than a film. Surprising plot twists may lie ahead, as close as the next presidential election. Chapter Two describes some of the mainstream, bipartisan policies that would address the nation's most pressing challenges. Chapter Three outlines ways and means that might seat a supporter of those policies in the Oval Office.

CHAPTER TWO

THE OPPORTUNITY

*America is always in decline and is always about
to bounce back.*
—James Fallows, 2010

L ate twentieth-century America worked. In fact, it worked exceptionally well. Rising from the wreckage of the Depression followed by World War II, the US went from strength to strength, building a nation of unrivaled power and an economy that created unimaginable prosperity.

The playbook in Washington was simple—not easy, but simple. Following their election victories, presidents set out priorities for the nation, then worked, debated, and compromised their ways to bipartisan congressional and public support. Past accomplishments are too readily taken for granted and their messages forgotten in these fraught times. These postwar achievements deserve to be remembered, respected, and emulated if possible. These included the following:

- **1946–64:** reducing wartime debt
- **1948:** Marshall Plan
- **1954:** downfall of Senator Joseph McCarthy
- **1956:** interstate highway act
- **1961–69:** NASA and the lunar landing
- **1964–65:** civil rights acts
- **1970:** Clean Air Act
- **1981–2000:** return to economic growth after stagflation
- **1983:** Social Security rescue
- **1989:** fall of the Berlin wall
- **1991:** freeing Kuwait
- **1996:** welfare reform
- **1998–2001:** debt reduction

The party-centric perspective of 2023 reflexively classifies some of these as liberal accomplishments and others as conservative, but each was bipartisan to its core. Presidents Harry Truman and Eisenhower patiently chipped away at the formidable wartime debt. A conservative Republican Congress passed President Truman's Marshall Plan to rebuild Europe. President Eisenhower paved the way for the censure of Republican senator McCarthy, unanimously supported by Senate Democrats. Minority Leader Everett Dirksen artfully maneuvered President Johnson's 1964 Civil

Rights Act past a seemingly insurmountable Democratic filibuster. The Clean Air Act passed almost unanimously in both Houses of Congress. A bipartisan committee established by President Reagan crafted the Social Security rescue plan that passed comfortably in a strongly Democratic House. A Democratic Congress gave President Bush both authorization and standing ovations for leading the international coalition to free Kuwait. (Ovations for an opposing-party president now seem unimaginable. Opposing-party legislators have been openly contemptuous of each of the last four presidents, and they would fear for their partisan lives if seen applauding "the enemy.") President Clinton's promise to "end welfare as we know it" needed Speaker Gingrich's Contract with America to reach fruition. Deficits became surpluses with Democrats raising taxes and Republicans cinching the purse strings.

Kumbaya? Hardly—politics ain't beanbag. Tough but respectful negotiating through challenges to reach agreement? Absolutely—this is how Washington worked, when it still worked.

It is no coincidence that most of these accomplishments remained intact and continued to benefit the nation for years or even decades. Two-party parentage greatly enhances a law's survival prospects after the White House or Congress changes hands.

In each of these success stories, the president played a dual role, telling his congressional opponents what they had to give up and his congressional allies what would elude their grasp. More recent presidents have rarely embraced this need to compromise with opponents, preferring to insult them, or disappoint allies, preferring to pander to them. This tendency was already evident in the Bush 43 and Obama administrations, but it came to full fruition with Presidents Trump and Biden, and it shows every sign of worsening.

Ample opportunities exist for returning to civilized and effective governance. Commonsense positions, conducive to reason and compromise, exist for even the most challenging problems facing the nation, often commanding broad voter support. The next president need only lay claim to this common ground.

Inflation

Inflation is caused by too much money chasing after too few goods.—Milton Friedman

This is perhaps the best-known quotation in economics. Millions of Americans can recite it from memory. Too few of them draw federal paychecks.

For most of this century, America's only consistent economic policy has been stimulation. Fiscal stimulus—borrowing to pay for higher spending or lower taxes—puts more money in consumers' hands, which it soon leaves to chase goods. Likewise monetary stimulus. Low interest rates and loose bank regulation make it easy to borrow more money to buy more goods. Nonstop stimulus is a tried-and-true recipe for inflation.

Candidate Trump bragged that "I love debt." Voters should have believed him. In FY2019, the federal deficit spiked by 25 percent despite unemployment already below 4 percent and millions of job openings begging for applicants. Stimulating an economy already operating at full capacity is both pointless and reckless. The deficit was rising sharply again in 2020 even before the pandemic arrived, spawning several stimulus bailouts that drove government spending to unprecedented levels. The first of these was clearly needed; subsequent iterations looked increasingly like vote buying. Far from trying to control this cash hemorrhage, Trump complained bitterly that the December 2020 bailout, a paltry $900 billion, should have been twice as large, with Speaker Pelosi egging him on. Altogether, the Trump administration spent money and piled up debt faster than either the Obama or the Bush 43 administration—no mean feat. (See the following topic.)

Starting from these nosebleed spending levels, President Biden proposed mammoth further increases, beginning with another $1.9 trillion COVID stimulus package, in an economy fast approaching full capacity and experiencing labor shortages. This was clear overreach. Larry Summers, the former treasury secretary and leading economic adviser in the Obama administration, warned that inflation would inevitably follow this feckless spending. Democrats wasted little time pondering that risk, or any other. President Biden signed the COVID stimulus bill *fifteen days* after it was first introduced in the House, reveling in Democrats' newfound partisan power to pass anything, with or without a coherent rationale. This works out to more than $100 billion of expenditures per day of deliberation, surely a record even in the world capital of spending other people's money.

After passage of the Bipartisan Infrastructure Bill, the rest of BBB ($3.5 trillion—"How big can we go?") met a different fate, and deservedly so. Republicans unanimously opposed this proposal. The filibuster rules of the Senate would prevent passage, so Democrats resorted to a reconciliation process, seeking 51–50 approval to hammer it through. From the outset, Senator Joe Manchin objected to the inflation risk, among other problems. Minor tweaks failed to allay his concerns. Manchin faced pressure and derision for his breach of party solidarity, but his determined opposition effectively killed the bill. A Democratic senator from a Republican state became the *one-person center* in rejecting the far left's spending agenda. It was a near-run thing.

The subsequent eruption of inflation even without BBB validated Summers' prediction and Manchin's concerns. Without Manchin's timely stand, that inflation would have been much higher and harder to unwind. No economist seriously doubts this.

Meanwhile, the Federal Reserve was on a perpetual dovish mission, holding the federal funds rate at essentially zero for nine of the thirteen years from 2009 through 2021, which attracted plenty of borrowers. Near zero was apparently too high for Trump, who repeatedly harangued the Fed to follow the European and Japanese lead on still lower interest rates, including negative interest. On top of this, the Fed undertook quantitative easing, basically longer-term debt purchases designed to suppress interest rates and encourage home-buying after the housing collapse. It worked, increasing the size and price of homes, but continued long after any need had passed. By 2021 the Fed had expanded its balance sheet by $8 trillion—that is, it had injected an extra $8 trillion into the economy to chase the same goods.

All this extra money busily confirmed Friedman's adage, translating directly into inflation, which soon exceeded 5 percent. Both Federal Reserve Chair Jerome Powell and Treasury Secretary Janet Yellen dismissed this spike as "transitory," which was correct in a perverse sense—inflation was transiting to much higher levels, topping out at over 9 percent in 2022. This wishful thinking delayed the needed course change in monetary policy for nearly a year. In the meantime COVID had disrupted supply chains, and Russia's Ukraine invasion significantly worsened the problem by taking natural gas and grain supplies off the global market.

The outcome has been all too predictable.[1]

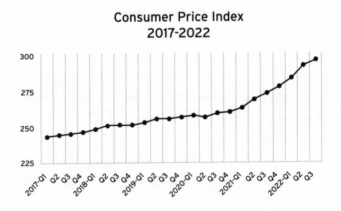

Consumer Price Index 2017-2022

Prices rose steadily from early 2017, taking only a single-quarter dip during the COVID recession in 2020. The series of COVID stimulus packages and overly accommodative Federal Reserve policies then accelerated inflation dramatically over the following two years. Another burst of preelection government spending in 2022 has only made the Fed's job harder, piling on more fiscal stimulus that partially counteracted monetary restraint. The White House and Congress showed they had no intention of exercising budgetary discipline to support the Fed's inflation fighting, sending a mixed message to the market. Private sector observers, usually fans of fiscal stimulus, were not confused about the likely outcome. As JPMorgan Chase CEO Jamie Dimon observed in Senate testimony, "I don't think you can spend $6 trillion and not expect inflation."

Polls consistently ranked inflation as a top public concern throughout 2022. Neither Trump nor Biden accepted any responsibility for the fiscal and monetary excesses that fed the worst inflation in forty years. Voters appear to hold Biden's administration primarily accountable. The approval ratings for his handling of inflation have been lower than for any other issue throughout 2022.[2]

Inflation and its corrective measures unavoidably inflict pain, sometimes over extended periods, as they did in 1978–82. The Federal Reserve pounded away with seven consecutive rate increases in 2022 while beginning gradual shrinkage of its balance sheet, with modest tangible progress through November 2022. Eventually, this regimen always works, though at the cost of lost jobs and bankruptcies of thinly capitalized firms. Recession is a common hangover, and most observers expect it in 2023.

Reversing Friedman's adage would avoid future bursts of inflation: create less money and more goods. The next president must appoint Federal Reserve governors who prioritize the commitment to a sound and stable currency by controlling the money supply and maintaining market interest rates. Fiscal and monetary prudence must operate in tandem rather than in conflict. Most Americans favor balanced budgets, at least in the abstract, but modest deficits (with a *B*, not a *T*) are also within the mainstream. This requires the president to exercise spending restraint, collect more taxes, or most likely both. See the following topic.

"More goods" means prioritizing work and productivity using commonsense measures. With the Ukraine invasion disrupting global and especially European oil and gas markets, it makes sense for US policy to encourage, not discourage, more domestic energy production, especially comparatively clean natural gas. Most Americans believe that President Biden should slow the transition away from fossil fuels in the current circumstances while laying the groundwork for a low-carbon future (see "Climate Change and Energy" below). With the threat of food shortages and a worsening drought in the western US, this is also a bad time to increase farm subsidies. Tariffs to protect domestic suppliers raise consumer prices. And so on.

A sustained labor shortage has been a longer-term contributor to the shortfall in output. Beginning in the Trump administration, the US has consistently had many more job vacancies (V) than unemployed workers (U) to fill them, reversing the norm. Economists use this V/U ratio to quantify labor tightness. It has lingered at record levels since 2021, as high as 2:1, which drove job-hopping and persistent wage inflation. This is predominantly a labor supply rather than demand problem; the number of new job openings being created has been fairly typical of a recovery from recession, but America lacks the willing workers to fill them.

COVID gets much of the blame for this labor shortage, but this chart from the St. Louis Federal Reserve also shows a troubling longer-term trend: fewer Americans are participating in the labor force—that is, either working or looking for work.

America on Strike?

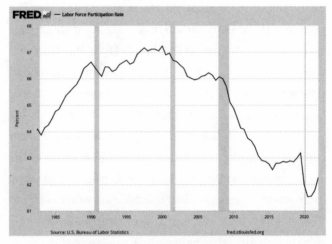

Source: U.S. Bureau of Labor Statistics   fred.stlouisfed.org

*Shaded areas indicate U.S. recessions

Growing labor force participation was a magic elixir for the US economy and wage income after 1982, reaching a high of 67 percent in 2000. By 2022 it had fallen to 62.2 percent. The *un*employment rate of 3.5 percent in August 2022 was identical to that before the start of the pandemic. The difference over those thirty months is the rise in *non*employment as a lifestyle choice, with three million fewer workers. Fewer young men (ages 20–24) chose to enter the workforce post-pandemic, raising labor economists' fears of a sustained trend. A declining work ethic would inevitably reduce output.

Several factors contributed since 2000. Broad early-retirement benefits, regardless of need, enticed many preseniors to stop working sooner than they might have intended. See "Rescuing Social Security" below. Ever-expanding grants and loans for college education delayed young Americans' entry into the job market. Higher education may confer an economic benefit—by supporting higher productivity and incomes after graduation—but it serves little purpose when graduates work as baristas. A full 40 percent of recent grads work at jobs that require only a high school diploma. Earlier retirement and later entry into the job market combined to shorten the average working life by years. Americans receiving disability benefits jumped by a quarter between 2007 and 2015. The Trump administration's anti-immigration bias shrunk the influx of foreign workers. See "Immigration and Border Security" below. Government subsidies and mandates discouraged work for too long during the pandemic: millions of job openings went begging, the supply chain suffered, and prices soared. COVID also disabled five hundred thousand workers long term.[3] Taken together, labor shortages and rising wages became stubborn contributors to the surge in inflation.

The fringes of both parties have cared more about promoting political agendas than about preventing or ending inflation. Neither party has committed to the concrete measures that would matter. Most American voters would embrace a candidate who placed a priority on rolling back inflation and assuring stable prices going forward.

Deficits and Debt

The principle of spending money to be paid by posterity
. . . is but swindling futurity on a large scale.
—Thomas Jefferson, 1816

As this century dawned, America's debt had fallen to post-WWII lows, thanks largely to the combined efforts of President Clinton and Speaker Gingrich.[4] President Bush 43 then broke the previous record for average annual deficits. President Obama broke that record. President Trump broke that record. And President Biden's first two years in office broke that record. With a combined deficit for the next two years projected to exceed $2.5 trillion, Biden's deficit for the four-year term will easily exceed any other four years in the nation's history.

These deficits piled onto the nation's debt. Entering 2023, America's debt burden reached an all-time high, with debt held by the public roughly equaling the nation's gross domestic product. Based on existing policies, the

Congressional Budget Office projects that debt will continue rising much faster than GDP, adding to the burden.

This was no tragic fiscal accident. Each of these administrations proudly announced their spendthrift intentions. Vice President Dick Cheney famously said that "deficits don't matter." Obama's treasury secretary Tim Geithner exulted that "the debate is over—there is no more focus on austerity." (The preceding trillion-dollar deficits had evidently reflected that "focus on austerity.") President Trump declared himself the "King of Debt" and earned that crown by returning to trillion-dollar deficits amid a robust economy (despite multiple campaign promises to balance the budget). When President Biden addressed spending bills by asking staffers, "How big can we go?" the answer came back: "Scary big." Major new spending programs included the American Rescue Plan ($1.9 trillion), Bipartisan Infrastructure Bill ($550 billion in added expenditures), CHIPS and Science Act ($280 billion), Inflation Reduction Act (pre-2024 election spending of $150–$200 billion, unknown thereafter), and the executive orders suspending and forgiving student loan payments ($426 billion, with unquantified more to come).

Updating Everett Dirksen's quip, "a trillion here, a trillion there, and pretty soon you're talking about real money."

Congress was complicit in spilling this red ink, but

these presidents bear the primary responsibility for the nation's burgeoning debt. They rarely opposed and essentially never vetoed congressional spending bills. The Trump White House sometimes conceded more spending to congressional Democrats to secure the votes needed to pass his own pet spending increases, a double whammy. In the Biden administration, it was Congress that applied spending "restraint" in 2021 (by the narrowest of margins), over the president's vehement objections, only to reopen the spigot as the midterms approached. It is the president's job to squelch and, if needed, veto excessive spending, not to encourage it.

These presidents, like many before them, have claimed that their spending would strengthen America's economy, offsetting the cost. History offers such examples, including the Louisiana Purchase, railroad land grants, the Tennessee Valley Authority, electrification, dams, the interstate highway system, air traffic control, and scientific research funding, but they are rare. Little of the twenty-first-century spending has resembled this kind of investment. It has been "here today, gone tomorrow" money: short-term splurges paid for with stubborn long-term debt. This debt weakens the economy, lowers living standards, and burdens the nation indefinitely.

Deficits may also be countercyclical: when demand is low, fiscal stimulus raises output closer to capacity.

Whether such deficits are efficient is frequently debated, but the question is moot here: the huge deficits in 2005–7, 2012–16, 2018–19, and 2021–22 only juiced up economies already operating near their short-term limits, which drives up spending with little potential output gain. Keynes spun in his grave.

These two decades provide an ample real-world test of systemic deep deficits as fiscal policy. This century has seen a steady decline in America's economic standing in the world. America's national debt grew year by year while the nation's share of global GDP fell, as the following graph illustrates.[5]

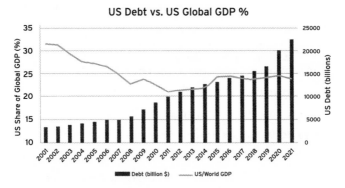

US deficit spending has stimulated the economic growth of China and other rivals far more than America's. Rising debt combined with a weakening economy is the worst-of-both-worlds outcome. Based on these curves, presidents of both parties get failing grades on their macroeconomic and budgetary policies.

Voters sometimes ask, in all sincerity, Who will pay these debts? They need only look in the mirror or at their children. Washington incurred these debts; Americans will pay them. No international bailout or other tooth fairy will come to the rescue. This repayment most likely takes the form of perpetual interest payments rather than actual principal payoffs of creditors, but this scarcely matters. *Paying interest forever is just another form of debt repayment, with the loan term set to infinity.* If anything, partial-principal payments over time would lessen rather than increasing the debt burden.

Negligible interest rates on federal debt masked this fiscal pain for more than a decade, but those rates were artificial, resulting from the Federal Reserve's capital market moves in response to the Great Recession. The Fed suppressed interest rates to encourage capital investments and recovery of real estate markets. These rates were never intended to last as long as they did, much less forever. Reality resumed in 2022. With aggregate net interest on the federal debt now projected to reach $60 trillion over the next thirty years,[6] a gross average of $2 trillion per year, the cost of perpetual interest repayment will be a palpable burden for every taxpayer, but especially millennials, who will pay this bill for their entire working lives.

These consistently deep deficits tie the hands of Washington policymakers. Rising debt service, much of it paid to foreign creditors, eats into available funds with no benefit to the citizenry. (More precisely, people have already enjoyed and forgotten any benefits of bygone deficit spending.) Infrastructure, research, and other longer-term discretionary initiatives go begging while revenues fall so far short of existing expenditures. Insolvent Social Security and Medicare trust funds cannot be rescued by a general fund already deeply in the red.

The sheer magnitude of America's national debt presents two threats beyond annual budget problems and generational equity. First, the dollar may lose its global status as the world's principal medium of exchange. The US could be tempted to lighten its debt burden by inflating away some of the dollar's value or even by repudiating some portion of that debt. The threat of either measure could persuade large creditors like China to promote an alternative reserve currency, which would significantly reduce America's influence in the world and alter the global economy in unpredictable ways, few of them likely to be positive.

Second, excessive debt may trigger a sovereign debt crisis, where lenders lose confidence in Treasury notes as risk-free investments and refuse to renew loans, and the government cannot cover these principal rollovers and interest payments as they come due. These are rare events in developed economies, but the recent euro crisis proved them possible, with Greece, Spain, Portugal, and Ireland suffering severe hardships while Italy and Belgium teetered on the edge, and Germany footed most of the bill. In the US, sustained spending excesses plus trillion-dollar interest bills piled on top of the already unprecedented debt level could quickly qualify as a crisis, with harsh corrective measures, all currently unimaginable, suddenly on the table.

Voters never clamored for deficits of this magnitude, and mainstream opinion strongly supports a return to fiscal sobriety before a crisis begins. The Biden administration's spending initiatives became less popular as their true cost began to emerge. Polls show a majority of all voters supporting a return to balanced budgets, which no twenty-first-century administration has even considered.

Few economists endorse a mandated balanced budget, largely because it fails to allow for exigencies like foreign military engagements or acts of nature (e.g., the COVID epidemic) or for economically constructive measures like countercyclical spending or new infrastructure investment.

Subject to such qualifications, the only responsible future direction is to stop digging the debt hole. Annual deficits must decline sharply, even if they never reach zero. Debt held by the public declining as a percentage of GDP is the best indicator of budgetary sobriety. Uninterrupted binge spending without offsetting revenue growth has damaged the United States profoundly, requiring corrective action that neither party's leadership has been willing to consider, because it would have crimped their largesse with other people's money.

The 1990s provide a handy template for trimming Washington's budgetary excesses: increase revenue and cut spending. The bipartisan welfare reform of 1996 provided a notable example of both. Structural changes in the welfare entitlement expanded the number of women in the workforce (more tax revenue) while lowering the number of welfare checks (less expense) and reducing childhood poverty drastically (better outcomes). The current bloated budget offers abundant targets of opportunity. One example: "temporary" Medicaid expansions to cope with the COVID public health emergency produce federal government outlays for otherwise ineligible individuals exceeding $100 billion annually. By universal admission, COVID ceased to be an emergency epidemic some time in 2021, yet the Biden administration extended the emergency declaration again in October 2022—little wonder in the month before midterm elections that appeared to be trending against Democrats. Hundreds of billions saved in cutting such expenditures would soon begin to make a difference.

Polls indicate that a presidential candidate with a commitment and a plan to end the runaway deficits would fare well with moderate and centrist voters. The 1992 election offers an encouraging precedent: independent Ross Perot gathered nearly twenty million votes, about half those of incumbent George H. W. Bush, running almost entirely on a balanced-budget platform. This sent a message to both parties that generated a sustained surplus beginning just six years later. The deficits and debt are now multiples of their 1992 levels, and the 2024 electorate has declared itself even more receptive to such a candidate.

Climate Change and Energy

A liberal society's ability to incubate innovation, technology, culture, and sustainable growth will determine the geopolitics of the future.
—Francis Fukuyama, 2022

Burning fossil fuels injects carbon dioxide into the atmosphere, where it traps infrared radiation, which warms the planet. More carbon dioxide, more warming. The air pollutants of the 1960s, though more hazardous in the short run, would dissolve in rainwater or decay chemically, so declining emissions translated quickly into declining pollution levels. Carbon dioxide is extremely stable, staying in the atmosphere for decades, which makes carbon emissions cumulative over many years. The world lives with these sins for a long time, which heightens the need to reduce new emissions. Everyone knows this, yet carbon abatement efforts have so far accomplished little at great expense. So, what to do?

This question has sharply divided the parties. President Obama championed the Paris Agreement. President Trump withdrew from that pact, supported a revival of coal power, and called global warming "mythical," "nonexistent," and "a hoax" "created by and for the Chinese." President Biden rejoined Paris and publicly attacked oil and gas companies, canceled pipelines, largely ended petroleum exploration and leasing on public lands, and appointed climate activists to a range of important administration posts. Cost be damned; we need to save the world. US climate change policy is a yo-yo, based solely on who is in power. Both extremes are wrong, leading to different dead ends at great cost, as most Americans intuitively understand.

Stubborn reliance on fossil fuels will inevitably continue carbon loading the atmosphere and warming the planet, with consequences that will become extreme, though not overnight. Dinosaurs roamed in subtropical Montana because the atmospheric carbon dioxide concentration was very high. Returning to that Cretaceous-period climate would have catastrophic consequences in the modern world. Climate change needs focused attention without delay.

Nevertheless, undermining America's existing energy arrangements before developing an affordable substitute fails for two basic reasons.

First, "cost be damned" may be a hit in Berkeley but it will not play in Poughkeepsie. As of October 2022, *80 percent* of Americans favored emphasizing energy independence and lower gasoline prices over climate change and higher gasoline prices.[7] Climate activists dismiss this preference as the product of gross ignorance, but democracy still means something. Moreover, the public's priorities rest on their own important reality: ample, cheap energy is a defining characteristic of all modern economies. Climate change deserves high-priority consideration, but nothing gets absolute precedence.

Americans will not sacrifice their economy or their living standards on this altar, and other developed nations tend to agree. The brave carbon dioxide abatement efforts undertaken by some European nations have had little practical impact on global warming while spiking energy prices beyond voters' tolerance. Germany and Denmark have consistently had electricity prices double those in the

US or more, with no end in sight. The average power-and-gas bill jumped 50 percent in Great Britain in 2022 alone, with more increases forecast, quickly ending the green-at-all-costs experiment. The British government announced a $170 billion subsidy to cap the energy cost increase, combined with reauthorization of fracking and a new round of North Sea drilling licenses. Shortly thereafter, Germany also adopted electricity and natural gas subsidies to keep businesses open and rescue consumers while slowing the phaseout of coal and nuclear, a tacit admission that the cost of *Energiewende* had simply gotten too high.

Using current technology, further growth in solar and wind energy produces too much power when it isn't needed and too little when it is. Alternating surpluses and shortages and the excess capital investments to maintain needed backup power sources are expensive. California's aggressive deployment of intermittent sources while decommissioning nuclear power plants has achieved soaring costs[8] along with sporadic power shortages extending indefinitely into the future, not precisely what Green New Deal advocates had promised and not an outcome that other states will emulate.

Most Americans accept the seriousness of climate change, but two-thirds oppose a sharp rise in energy costs and subsidies to deploy immature technologies, favoring instead a measured transition to clean power over time.[9] They reject both parties' extreme positions, presenting a clear opening for a moderate candidate in 2024.

Second, this show also flops in Beijing, and therefore globally. China under Chairman Xi looks to rule the world, not save it. His self-proclaimed destiny is "the eventual demise of capitalism and the ultimate victory of social-ism,"[10] that is, of course, Chinese socialism. That victory requires ample low-cost power to fuel economic growth. The following graph[11] shows the impact of China's policies on carbon dioxide emissions:

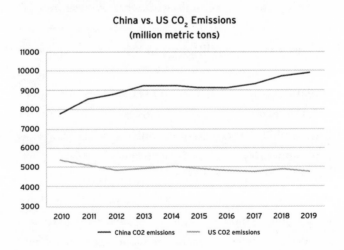

China vs. US CO_2 Emissions
(million metric tons)

China's emissions have risen fast, while US emissions have declined modestly.

The differentiator is coal. China continues building generators to burn its limitless cheap coal reserves, while the US has been shrinking its coal-fired power capacity. Altogether, US coal usage declined by nearly half from 2010 to 2019, while China's rose by 12 percent, by far the largest contributor to China's rising energy output and, even more so, its rising carbon dioxide emissions. This was a conscious decision: Xi assumed power in 2013; coal usage began rising (following an extended decline) in 2016.[12] China has become largely indifferent to its climate impact, in its deeds if not its words. Its priorities will not change, regardless of international suasion, because China is a nation in a hurry—it needs to get rich and powerful before its population ages too much to sustain rapid economic growth.[13]

Given trends in China, the rest of the world's carbon abatement fades nearly into insignificance. By some measures China's emissions exceeded those of *all developed economies combined* in 2022. China has been adding over 75 percent of the world's new coal-fired power capacity.[14] It is not constructing these power plants today to decommission them tomorrow. Whatever its public declarations, China is committed to coal for as long as it remains the cheapest source of power. Other underdeveloped nations are also embracing coal, for similar reasons. With the invasion of Ukraine exacerbating natural gas shortages, even advanced

Western European economies are mining and importing more coal to keep the lights on through the winter.

Burning pure carbon produces the highest ratio of carbon dioxide emissions per kilowatt-hour of power produced. Expanding global coal-generating capacity is therefore antithetical to any concept of progress against climate change. Any other energy source would be preferable, but even some well-intentioned nations have painted themselves into the proverbial corner with overly ambitious curtailment of less-bad sources. Despite all the goals, commitments, and expense, the planet is still warming, global emissions are increasing, and the hypothetical Intergovernmental Panel on Climate Change abatement pathways are increasingly detached from the reality of China.

A thought experiment clarifies the existing global warming/energy posture. Imagine the US going all in with implementation of existing green-energy technology, investing trillions of dollars and enacting severe restrictions to "achieve immediate, drastic annual emission reductions"— the Greta Thunberg prescription—with the goal of slashing America's carbon dioxide output by half in 2030, hoping, contrary to all the evidence, that this is even possible. This miracle would produce (1) a negligible deceleration in global warming (i.e., the planet would still be warming at nearly the same rate); (2) much more expensive energy, a weaker economy, and declining living standards in the US; and (3) a further shift in global power and influence toward China, with its continued reliance on cheap coal giving it an economic advantage. Most energy experts broadly agree with this prognosis, though they exercise more discretion in their public comments than displayed here.

The Paris Agreement is failing to achieve or even approach its goals. The COP26 and COP27 climate conventions were largely admissions of failure coupled with admonitions to try harder.[15] The World Meteorological Organization estimates that future emission reductions would need to be *four times* more ambitious than currently "committed" to stay below the two degrees Celsius global temperature-increase target.[16] And even those inadequate commitment levels are written in disappearing ink; they have never been met, except during the COVID lockdowns. Promises are cheap; results are expensive.

Paris cannot succeed because developing nations reject its global pain-sharing premise. Economic growth is their number one priority, to lift their populations out of poverty or enhance their global standing, and they will embrace carbon-free energy only when it enhances that growth. Let the rich countries solve the problem they caused. But lowering emissions in the US and Europe serves little purpose: while the developing world burns more coal, atmospheric carbon dioxide concentrations will continue rising, regardless of any other factor.

Real solutions must therefore be *economically* compelling so they play in Beijing and New Delhi as well as Poughkeepsie. That means *market-based green*—that is, energy options cheap enough to prevail with producers and consumers even apart from their environmental merits.

The Model T put America on wheels not because it was cheaper and better than other cars but because it was cheaper and better than horses. Carbon-free energy will take over China and India when it becomes cheaper and better than coal. From a climate change perspective, no other goal is even worth considering. From an energy perspective, this will be another major advance in a long history of leaps forward.

Past energy revolutions supplanted slave labor, oxen and horses, firewood, wind and water mills, and whale oil. These advances delivered more abundant, less expensive, cleaner, more useful, and more humane energy sources, transforming life in the developed economies. The next revolution must meet two added conditions: near-zero carbon emissions and suitability for less developed economies. Hard, but still possible.

Modernized nuclear power will be an important contributor. Passively safe reactor designs remove the risk of the radiation leakage that occurred at the Chernobyl, Three Mile Island, and Fukushima facilities. Nuclear power's fuel costs are minimal, yet the overall cost remains high, because up-front expenses and regulatory delays have often been exorbitant. The cost drivers have been part technological, part obstructive tactics by opponents, but the solution to both problems seems clear: mass production of highly standardized, proved, modular, and therefore uncontroversial designs. This yields manufacturing economies and eliminates the up-front cost of making each proposed installation into a novel engineering project. France pioneered standardized reactor designs decades ago. These reactors continue to generate power that is far cheaper and far cleaner than Germany's *Energiewende* experiment, even without the most current nuclear technologies.

France plans fourteen new reactors, while Germany, Japan, Belgium, and California have postponed or reconsidered their plans to phase out reactors. Venture capital investment poured into nuclear technology in 2021-22, accelerating innovation. Most Americans who are serious about addressing global warming recognize, whether reluctantly or enthusiastically, that nuclear energy must play a role. Nuclear power warrants (1) meaningful government support and coordination among technology leaders and utilities, and (2) streamlined regulatory paths and, if necessary, subsidies to begin deploying this vital, carbon-free continuous power supply. Virginia is exploring creation of an innovation zone for developing small modular reactor technologies, but the federal government will need to play a key role for nuclear power to be a timely part of a market-based green solution.

Wind and solar already provide cheap carbon-free power, and solar costs will decline further with the spread of higher-efficiency tandem and bifacial cells.[17] The problem is that both sources are intermittent, delivering power only when the wind blows or the sun shines, which in no way equates to continuous electricity on demand ("dispatchable" power). Intermittency requires extensive redundancy as the share of these renewable sources rises, making heavy reliance on intermittent power sources too expensive for market-based green energy.

Grid-scale storage converts intermittent into continuous power, just as reservoirs convert intermittent rain and snowfall into a continuous water supply, but existing storage options cost too much. Promising new grid-scale batteries should sharply lower these costs. The key is finding electrode materials that store charge for much longer than lithium (days or weeks versus hours) at a fraction of the cost. Iron-air and sodium-sulfur batteries are promising candidates, with the potential to reduce costs to as little as one or two cents per delivered kilowatt-hour with technology improvements and economies of scale. When combined with declining wind and solar generation expense, this could become more than competitive as a primary power source. More R & D investment is needed to convert that potential into reality.

This energy revolution will require other investments. The power grid must be upgraded to accommodate new power sources and expanded for charging millions of electric vehicles. Mobile batteries must improve to make those vehicles more affordable and practical. Air transport and ocean shipping need low-cost synthetic fuels. Cheap carbon recapture, most likely through bioengineering of plants, will be needed in the long run because atmospheric carbon dioxide concentrations are becoming higher than desirable and new emissions will never fall to zero.

The common theme is that current green technology is inadequate—it costs too much and delivers too little to wean the developing world off coal—but clean *and* economical energy is achievable with time and investment in the science and engineering.

Advanced technology costs money, but better to invest that money in cures than to fritter it away on Band-Aids and tokens. The US spends hundreds of times more on mandating or subsidizing solar and wind power

installations than on energy R & D. This is all for naught—
more turbines and solar panels in the US could not come
close to offsetting growing emissions in the developing
world. Voters who care about global warming need to
support solutions that China and India will actually imple-
ment. Anything else is an exercise in futility.

In the meantime, sensible half-a-loaf measures can
contain the extent of the future challenge without damaging the economy or lowering standards of living. Fracking
technology has made natural gas a useful bridge to a greener
future. The US reduced its power-generation emissions primarily by substituting shale gas for coal, and other nations
could do the same as an interim step without massive
investment. Improved fuel efficiency, plug-in hybrid vehicles, prevention and suppression of wildfires and coal seam
fires, smarter buildings, more insulation, reflective surfaces,
and other conservation measures could reduce emissions
substantially at little cost or modest inconvenience.

Climate change deniers reject this intermediate
approach because it recognizes climate change as a real
problem that needs prompt attention and public investment
to solve. Activists reject it for failure to treat climate change
as an existential crisis that subordinates all other considerations. Unilateral actions from the White House, siding
with one extreme or the other, have cost much time and

money. This situation cries out for presidential leadership *from the center* to enact comprehensive climate change *and* energy legislation with a sensible long-term focus.

Most mainstream voters are ready to start on this challenge by doing something practical and constructive now and working toward doing better later. A presidential aspirant espousing this kind of pragmatic approach might be rewarded with broad support.

Immigration and Border Security

He had expected labour, and he found it, and did it and made the best of it. In this, his prosperity consisted.
—Charles Dickens, 1859

Congress has considered three sensible immigration reforms over the last two decades: the Kennedy-McCain bill of 2006, the Kennedy-Kyl bill of 2008, and the bipartisan "Gang of Eight" proposal in 2013. None were perfect, all offered solid bases for negotiating immigration reform, and each died a horrible partisan death.[18] Speaker Dennis Hastert refused to bring the Kennedy-McCain bill to the floor, preferring to advance a House Republican bill with zero prospects for passage. Democratic senators (including

Obama, Clinton, Sanders, and Biden, two future presidents, one nominee, and one wannabe) euthanized the Kennedy-Kyl bill in an election year by passing a "poison pill" amendment gutting the guest worker program, the principal inducement for Republican support. Speaker John Boehner killed the 2013 reform, which had passed the Senate by a two-to-one margin and enjoyed majority House support, but less than majority *Republican* support. In each instance, Washington political leaders elevated party interests and loyalty over the urgent national priority of comprehensive immigration reform. Since then, no serious immigration proposal has been advanced.

With no appetite for compromise in DC, America must continue to deal with a hot mess on its southern border combined with too few legal immigrants to support America's economy and ensure its future, the worst of all possible worlds.

Mainstream America supports two fundamental immigration concepts:

1. America must continue welcoming new citizens from around the globe. Immigrants of every nationality, race, and religion have found their way to the US, fleeing hardship or seeking opportunity. Each new wave took its turn being oppressed and demeaned, but those new Americans enriched the nation over time. (One striking

example: immigrants or their children had founded 40 percent of all the Fortune 500 companies in 2012.) In recent decades immigrants from Mexico, Central America, and Asia have supplied the US economy with a much-needed pool of labor, skills, and brainpower. They have also borne and raised more than their share of children, sparing America from Japan's geriatric spiral.

2. America also needs secure borders. The essential purpose of national borders is to restrict who is allowed in a country and on what terms. Nations are not altruistic entities, committed to self-sacrifice for the greater global good. Barring exceptional circumstances, America's first allegiance is to Americans. Every nation can and must decide how many and which foreigners it wants to welcome, based on its self-interest and the welfare of its citizens. Only secure borders give those invitations meaning. Borders cannot distinguish among future Americans, undocumented workers, moochers, drug mules, and violent criminals. They are secure against all or none, to be crossed only with America's permission.

President Trump and many right-wing Republicans neither comprehend nor respect the first concept. Much of their rhetoric has been unthinkingly anti-immigrant or antiforeigner, too often with insulting or racial overtones. Legal immigration fell each year of the Trump administration, even as record low unemployment and a rising number of unfilled job slots screamed out for more workers. The denial rate for highly skilled individuals (H-1B petitions) soared from 6 percent in 2015 to 30 percent in 2020.[19] That is, the administration was systematically turning away willing and able applicants for existing job openings during a labor shortage.[20] No rational interpretation of "America First" would support this willful denial of the nation's economic self-interest. This cumulative loss persists into 2023. Pending onset of a likely recession, America still has many more job openings than it has workers to fill them, a condition that labor market economists would have deemed impossible even a decade ago. This contributed to soaring prices beginning in 2021, it substantially drove the Federal Reserve's tightening policy in 2022, and it undermines the prospects for declining interest rates or sustained economic growth.

Most moderates and independents strongly disapproved of President Trump's chest-thumping treatment of immigration.[21]

President Biden and many left-wing Democrats neither understand nor respect the second concept. AOC seeks to end immigration enforcement entirely, selling "Abolish ICE" T-shirts on her website. Immediately upon candidate Biden winning the election, Central American and Cuban emigrants began surging toward the border in record numbers. A tiny portion of these pose a threat of violence against America. Dozens of aliens in the FBI's Terror Suspect Database have begun to be apprehended in the empty wastes between border-crossing checkpoints, a long-feared security threat first observed in 2021. Terrorist wannabes can apparently follow American news and react to changes in Washington.

More broadly, these uninvited migrants as a group have no special skills or attributes that would recommend them as future Americans. With no opportunities in their home countries, they hoped to find better prospects to the north—understandable, but not a wish that immigration laws are written to grant. Their chances of ever receiving green cards are slim to none under existing laws and guidelines. Record numbers therefore decided to seek asylum instead—that is, they claim to fear "serious harm" due to "persecution" in their home countries.[22] This is largely a pretext. These legal criteria for refugee status are quite narrow and do not include the economic hardships that motivate most of these applicants. Nevertheless, the Biden administration reversed prior policy by admitting over one million asylum seekers into America, pending hearings on their applications (as of August 2022).[23] This is roughly ten times the upper limit that could be granted asylum under American law, casting doubt on the rationale for this policy change. The likely outcome is all too predictable. Few applicants who trekked hundreds of miles to enter America based on spurious claims will voluntarily return to their homelands when their applications are eventually denied.

The southern border states have naturally borne the brunt of this surge, especially Texas and Arizona. Vice President Harris was assigned the task of investigating the border-state problem and cavalierly blew it off. Frustrated by the administration's inaction, those border states began busing thousands (a fraction of 1 percent) of these uninvited immigrants to New York City; Washington, DC; and other sanctuary cities, provoking their mayors into strenuous objections and pleas for financial support. New York City mayor Eric Adams declared a state of emergency due to the influx of 17,000 new immigrants transported from the border. Those additional dependents undoubtedly place real burdens on New York, but compare those to the problems of Yuma, Arizona, population 100,000, with 250,000 new undocumented immigrants passing through. *That* is an emergency.[24]

Those Republican governors have rightly been accused of a publicity stunt in busing these immigrants, but they made their point: porous borders look much better when viewed from a safe distance. Within two months after immigrant busing began, the Biden administration struck a deal with Mexico to take and house Venezuelan refugee applicants pending their hearings in the US, and the pace of busing slowed sharply. Unfortunately, the respite at the border proved fleeting.

The border situation has begun to alarm a broad cross section of Americans. In an August 2022 NPR poll, 73 percent of respondents expressing an opinion thought it "completely true" or "somewhat true" that the US is experiencing an "invasion" at its southern border, including slimmer majorities among Democrats and independents.[25] Only 37 percent of Americans approved of President Biden's handling of immigration as of September 2022, his second-lowest approval rating on any issue.[26]

Blinded by their ideologies and in thrall to their fringes, both parties ignore the simple truths of immigration. Unmanaged or mismanaged, it is a national problem, as the last six years and the border mess bear witness. Properly managed, having millions of people around the globe vying to become Americans is an asset, not a liability. The ability to select skilled or highly educated workers to fill the nation's needs and strengthen the domestic production of its companies, with training and education paid for by others, has long been the envy of the world. Mexico trains an electrician, who then immigrates to the US. Which country should feel disgruntled over that?

President Trump's famous rally line—"when Mexico sends its people, they're not sending their best"—is gibberish, reflecting no comprehension of the process. Mexico does not forcibly expel its citizens to the US; the individuals decide to emigrate and where they want to go. A Mexican electrician applies to live and work in America where more lucrative job opportunities await, and America approves or denies the application. And some of these legal migrants surely *have been* among Mexico's best, judging from their successes here. The problem is gate crashers, but that problem has become too large to be ignored or whitewashed. Most Americans understand that, even if their leaders do not.

Immigration helped build America's economic preeminence for generations. Chinese immigrants largely built the early western railroads. World War II and its aftermath brought thousands of European scientists and engineers to the US, which soon became the world leader in almost every field of technology, from semiconductors to birth control. Central and South America have provided the labor to support America's stunningly productive agribusiness. The US would have prospered without them, but it prospered mightily with them.

Any leader searching for common ground on immigration need not look far.[27] Most Americans embrace resident foreigners who apply legally, bring needed skills and support themselves, and "become American," for example, by integrating into their communities. Large numbers of immigrants will be welcomed as long as jobs await them. Law-abiding Dreamers, technically illegal but blameless, are welcome to stay and continue their lives in the only country they have ever known. Refugees from war-torn countries (e.g., Afghanistan and Ukraine) are also welcome on a humanitarian basis, as part of a global response. Most Americans favor a path to citizenship for legal aliens and have been known to join with their immigrant friends to celebrate their naturalization papers. Those new Americans strengthen the nation while enhancing their own prospects.

The opposite consensus emerges at the open-border end of the policy spectrum. Americans had little patience with fifteen thousand Haitians who crossed the Rio Grande into Del Rio, Texas, then refused to leave, or Central American caravans that bullied their ways through Mexico to the US border demanding entry. American citizenship is a privilege for immigrants, not a right. Mutual benefit is the litmus test. Immigrants get invited by bringing something to the party; crashers must be firmly invited to leave for that invitation to have meaning.

Within that broad framework, dozens of details remain for the political process to resolve. The point for current purposes is that more lawful immigration combined with a secure border offers palpable gains for both existing and new Americans. A presidential candidate committed to that middle ground will help unite the nation and gain popularity in the process. The prevailing dogmas of left and right, open borders versus impenetrable wall, will produce only more animosity and a weaker America.

National Security

Politics stops at the water's edge.
—Arthur Vandenberg, 1948

The American people generally believe the world is safer, and that we are safer, when we are stronger.
—Jeane Kirkpatrick

Political polarization has drastically weakened America's military and diplomatic standing in the world in just two decades. The nation finds itself deeply divided while facing global challenges unimaginable when the Berlin Wall fell or following Desert Storm. Domestic unity and a return to core principles are prerequisites for the US to regain its preeminent role in international security and foreign affairs.

"To provide for the common defence" was a bedrock commitment of the Constitution, but national security has now morphed into global security, extending far beyond existential threats to America. The Allies' defeat of Axis dictators in World War II finally replaced the traditional right of conquest with a right of national self-determination, which is memorialized in the United Nations Charter ("All Members shall refrain in their international relations from the threat or use of force against the territorial integrity or political independence of any state . . ."). NATO and numerous other treaties and security compacts followed, all to the same effect. "The common defense" took on a global meaning, with US military might as the linchpin in resisting dictators intent on expansion and oppression of weaker neighbors.

Desert Storm epitomized this commitment. Saddam Hussein coveted the oil of Kuwait, so he invaded the country and occupied it. This threatened to destabilize the region and give Iraq dangerous leverage in Middle Eastern and even global affairs. A thirty-five-nation coalition led by the US liberated Kuwait in a hundred-hour ground war with an almost surreal (and very gratifying) display of America's military technology, hardware, and training.

President Bush's simple and confident declaration that "this will not stand" was predicated on his trust that Congress would approve a military intervention, which it did, despite sizable Democratic majorities in both Houses. Authorizations, funding, and verbal support flowed smoothly and with little drama in the run-up to hostilities, fostering a public consensus on the need for action. The military carried out its mission with high transparency and low casualties.

Three American assets assured this decisive result in Desert Storm: domestic cohesion, solid alliances, and clear technological superiority over any and all rivals. At the time, few even imagined that any of those would prove transitory. Three decades on, not one of those assets still looks secure.

America's political polarization weakens the nation's alliances because presidents can only count on their own parties' support for action against anything less than existential threats. This deep and seemingly perpetual political division also compromises the "rally 'round the flag" effect that has generally supported foreign military operations. Too many Americans refuse to support an opposing party's president as a matter of habit and for fear of bolstering his position politically. Even if subconsciously, some Americans might prefer that the nation appear weak over an opposing-party president appearing strong.

The Ukraine conflict could become a case in point. In October 2022, Kevin McCarthy issued a thinly veiled threat to deny support to Ukraine, which would nearly assure the success of Russia's invasion. A week later, a letter from the Progressive Caucus led by Representative Jayapal urged President Biden "to seek realistic terms for a ceasefire," a move that would undermine Ukrainian president Volodymyr Zelenskyy and embolden Putin's expansionist ambitions. Mainstream Democrats promptly demanded and received a retraction, but the message had already been sent and received: fringes of the two parties might make common cause, albeit for disparate reasons, to cut off funding for Ukraine.

This kind of domestic divisiveness is enough in itself to undermine American influence abroad. The US need not actually renege on commitments to lose the trust of allies. Coalition partners sensing that US involvement may depend on the results of the next election are less likely to commit for fear of being left holding the bag. Opposing forces are commensurately less fearful of America's involvement and more willing to play the long game, holding out for divisions in Washington to sap their enemy's will. Political partisanship thus encourages the nation's adversaries while discouraging its allies.

Allies' confidence in America has been severely shaken in recent years. Obama was broadly popular overseas, but his "lead from behind" policy unsettled allies accustomed to actual American leadership. ("Leading" and "behind" are antonyms.) Trump was not merely critical of NATO and the leadership of other NATO members; he openly urged American withdrawal from the organization, a gift that would have exceeded Putin's wildest dreams. The expression of this isolationist view combined with undertones of Trump's "America First" slogan embold- ened America's enemies while leaving allies wondering how to hedge their bets. Biden labeled Saudi Arabia, a key Mideast ally since World War II, a "pariah." He saw "very little redeeming value in the present government in Saudi Arabia" and halted arms sales to the Saudis. The predict- able chilling effect enabled Russia to make opportunistic inroads with OPEC and the Gulf Coast states. The Saudis' relations with China have also warmed.[28]

America's internal discord and weakening influence with allies have emboldened its enemies. Two expansion- ist dictators are setting the global foreign policy agenda, blatantly flouting their nations' UN Charter commitments. Putin openly seeks to reconstitute the Soviet Union. He has already annexed Georgia, Crimea, and parts of Ukraine with actual or threatened military invasions and shows no indication of stopping voluntarily. Xi is trying to transform the South China Sea into a Chinese lake and openly flaunts his plans to annex Taiwan, the eighteenth-largest economy in the world, by invasion if necessary. Much of China's defense budget is dedicated to preparations for that invasion. Xi sees a short-term window of opportunity that will likely close as China's population ages and its economic growth wanes.[29] The Taiwanese want no part of becoming the next Hong Kong but justifiably wonder whether the world's democracies will protect their right to choose against a nuclear and conventional military power as formidable as China. Without decisive American leadership along the lines of Desert Storm, the answer would certainly be a regretful "no." And without enforcement, that right, like any other, becomes meaningless.

The Ukraine conflict exemplifies the critical importance of permanent military alliances. A Western coalition built from scratch with Russian tanks already rolling would likely have proved too little too late. Instead, Ukraine's elite forces had developed their tactics in exercises with NATO member forces. The NATO infrastructure enabled the timely delivery of advanced weaponry from multiple sources, partially equalizing the vast disparity in troop levels, helicopters, and artillery.

Compared to Desert Storm, this has been a modest

effort, conducted by proxy, and the results reflect it. Russia's invasion has been contained and in places repelled, but not defeated. The final resolution remains much in doubt. Still, NATO nations' involvement kept the principle of national self-determination intact, even if compromised. Though badly outnumbered, Ukraine has used Western military technology and training to thwart Russian forces, contrary to most expectations.

The Ukrainians' willingness to endure, fight, and sacrifice beyond those expectations may discourage aggressors and encourage this kind of US assistance in the future. Even imperfect allies are worth supporting if the alternative is appeasement of expansionist dictators. The NATO membership applications of Sweden and Finland show a heightened willingness to oppose Russia's territorial appetite by those on the front line, whatever doubts they may harbor about America. Frustrating Putin's ambitions may also have delivered a salutary message to the Russian people. Putin's mobilization of three hundred thousand marginal troops and threats of resorting to nuclear weapons may be undermining his previously unassailable domestic support.

China's threatened invasion of Taiwan would much more severely test American military superiority and political will. With the help of industrial espionage, China has diligently pursued robotic mini-submarines, hypersonic missiles, ground-based and orbital satellite killers, fifth-generation fighter jets, and other advanced military technologies, enough to offset some remaining American advantages. China likely possesses the second most capable conventional military forces on the planet, though still untested in serious combat.

A determined invasion by the Chinese would require direct military involvement by the US and its allies, with a high cost in blood and treasure, but the alternative would also be ugly. Teaching Xi that the US will give way when the cost gets high potentially carries an even steeper price tag over time. If China succeeded in annexing Taiwan by force, the right of national self-determination would be a dead letter, at least as applied to potent military powers. China would have a nearly free hand in East Asia, with its many emerging economies. America's unwillingness or inability to prevent the invasion would severely debase its global standing and global currency in high-tension regions. As Xi's threats have become more bellicose, American public opinion has trended toward favoring some form of military involvement in Taiwan if needed.

In contrast to all the domestic discord over so many issues, Americans' support for their armed forces has rarely been stronger. Polls repeatedly identify the military as the most respected American institution by far—nearly

90 percent of those expressing an opinion view the military favorably.[30] Parents take pride in their children in uniform, and veterans are widely respected and thanked for their service.

This public support comes with some limitations. Americans expect their armed forces, including their commander in chief, to stay within certain boundaries, including the following:

Defined and achievable objectives: The bitter memory of Vietnam still lingers. Desert Storm enjoyed strong bipartisan support from beginning to end because President Bush defined the mission clearly—expel Iraqi forces from Kuwait—and recalled American forces when they had accomplished that mission. Bush 43's invasion of Iraq, in contrast, morphed from removing weapons of mass destruction to regime change to nation building, the last proving to be a bridge too far, with little apparent reflection on the changing balance between costs and benefits. America's goals in the Ukraine conflict would benefit from more concrete definition.

Reasonable expense: America spends more on its military than any other nation, and that budget can generate domestic friction. Nothing in the budget deserves a blank check, not even national defense. All three branches have too many flag officers (generals and admirals) and too many meaningless bases for a streamlined modern military, both entailing excessive overhead expense. Endless government-funded development programs often die of old age and exhaustion without ever deploying new weapons, or they produce systems that are unaffordable in the numbers needed to be effective. More "skunk works" and private sector–based programs are needed.

Integration with allies: America is the logical and essential military leader of the free world, but leading is quite different from going it alone. If America's staunch allies demur or disengage from a meaningful military undertaking, the public naturally and often rightly begins to question its wisdom.

America's global stature is not ordained. It must be earned, domestically and internationally. Recent presidents have failed in that duty. A mainstream candidate pledging to maintain the nation's military prowess, and to use it to defend the US, its allies, and the principle of national self-determination, can expect broad voter support.

Rescuing Social Security

*You cannot escape the responsibility of tomorrow
by evading it today.*
—Abraham Lincoln, 1862

*In a time of deceit, telling the truth is
a revolutionary act.*
—George Orwell

Voters do not yet include the future of Social Security among the important issues facing America. They should, and they will when politicians acknowledge the program's fragile state, but that may happen too late to avoid unnecessary hardship.

Through its long history, Social Security has saved millions of older Americans from poverty and has often ranked as the most popular federal program. In this century, however, the program has drifted out of sync with reality and with its core purpose. Recent administrations have chosen to ignore the looming problems and mislead the American people regarding their magnitude and urgency. That deception ends soon, one way or another. Procrastination is no longer an option. If the next administration fails to act, Social Security's trustees will be forced to reduce benefit payments across the board.

In the Depression, the case for a comprehensive go-vernment-funded retirement program was compelling. Only 6 percent of the population had celebrated a 65th birthday, and few of those would celebrate many more. Many without jobs were in desperate straits, unable to afford housing or decent food. As unemployment soared, some employers applied financial triage to their workforces, pushing older jobholders aside in favor of younger men supporting fam-ilies. A Keynesian urge to create demand completed the picture. With so many to support so few, the burden was light. It was the perfect setting for a program to pay elders a living stipend on condition that they stop working.

Those circumstances have substantially reversed since then. The economy suffers not from too few jobs but from too few workers. Over 18 percent of Americans are age 65 or older, and most will live another decade or more. On average, they are wealthier than younger Amer-icans, and Census Bureau data show that their median incomes have risen far faster than any other age group's since 1967.[31] Depending on the measure used, around one-eighth of seniors live in poverty, although half or more may depend on their Social Security checks to make ends meet.[32] Between pensions, IRA distributions, and other investment income, along with Medicare to reduce and cap health-care expenses, many affluent elders have no real need for Social Security, having provided nicely for their own retirements. Their monthly checks may marginally augment their lifestyles, but at the expense of younger Americans who may never reach the income and wealth levels enjoyed by their parents.

If Social Security had never existed, creating it now in its current universal form would be sheer madness. Senior poverty is now the exception rather than the rule, calling for a narrower, means-based approach. Instead of adapting, the nation's costliest program remains mired in Depression-era stereotypes and lavish expenditures when moderation was needed.[33]

The original Social Security Act of 1935 contemplated the building of a large reserve to fund future benefits, the legally required approach for private sector retirement programs when undertaking commitments that stretch out for decades. That would have avoided the current crisis, but it lasted only four years before Congress spent the reserve to enlarge and accelerate benefits. When a sizable reserve reemerged by 1950, President Truman increased benefits and relaxed eligibility standards to consume it. The 1965 amendment siphoned off money to support disability insurance and expand benefits further. And so on. Program sweeteners win votes, and Washington will always find some use for loose cash. Costs can be counted later, often after the generous grantors of expanded benefits have left office.

Social Security today would be unrecognizable to President Roosevelt and the Seventy-Fourth Congress, but their successors found all the expansions sensible, or at least expedient, when seeking reelection. Successful entitlements grow, usually to the detriment of their own soundness.

Now the bills are coming due. Social Security benefits and administration cost $160 billion more than net payroll contributions yielded in 2021, up two-thirds from a $96 billion shortfall just four years earlier.[34] Since then, two huge cost of living benefit increases triggered by the inflationary surge are rapidly adding to that deficit, which is projected to grow to around $500 billion per year in 2030, another tripling over nine years. Rather than accumulating reserves against its unfunded future obligations, the Social Security Administration is sinking ever deeper in the red in its current operations.

This Social Security shortfall is an annual expense, not a one-off discretionary expenditure, at least while the trust fund lasts. There is no annual appropriation requiring congressional or executive approval. The law sets contribution, benefit, and eligibility rules. The program then costs what it costs, with any shortfall adding to the government's annual borrowing requirement. Full speed ahead and damn the torpedoes!

Such mandatory spending, consisting mostly of entitlements and interest on the debt, consumed roughly two-thirds of all federal tax revenue in 2022, up from less than half in 2000. This left just one-third of all revenue to cover national defense, the State Department, the federal courts, scientific research and the national labs, Congress, the White House, public parks and lands, employee pensions, the Commerce and Labor Departments, NASA, the IRS, FBI, CIA, EPA, CDC, FDA, SEC, and everything else. Trillion-dollar deficits are the predictable result. With the Social Security deficit and average interest rates on the debt both rising over the next decade, this budgetary bind worsens. As mandatory spending reaches three-quarters or more of all revenue, bond holders' anxiety can only increase.

Social Security in its current form also worsens the nation's labor shortage. The primary culprit is the early-retirement option at age 62, five years younger than full retirement age. This never made sense and certainly does not now. Retirement benefits were designed to provide for the elderly's waning years. Few Americans have waned all that much at 62. Extended life expectancies and longer vitality called for raising, not lowering, the retirement age, as the bipartisan 1983 reform bill recognized.

Predictably, the lure of early-retirement benefits has

proved irresistible—people will respond to incentives, and deferring gratification is hard. Over 40 percent of Americans begin taking Social Security benefits at 62, making it by far the most popular retirement age. Accepting those benefits practically mandates dropping out of the labor force—the alternative is a punitive 50 percent tax above a low earnings threshold.[35] The result is that two-thirds of all Americans leave the labor force altogether before their full retirement age of 67, exactly what an economy with an aging population profile does *not* need. What is supposed to be the norm has become an exception, and an exception intended to accommodate special circumstances has become the norm.

The COVID epidemic's "Great Retirement" worsened an already bad situation, at least temporarily. In the first two years of the epidemic, the number of retirees aged 55 and over rose by two million,[36] explaining much of the sharp drop in labor force participation (see the "America on Strike?" chart under "Inflation" above). Social Security's rules will make some of these early retirements especially "sticky." A retirement election can be withdrawn only within twelve months of the original application for benefits, only once in a lifetime, and only by refunding all benefits previously received, which proves awkward if the retiree has been living on those benefits. As of late 2022, the longer-term reduction of the workforce due to COVID is worrisome but hard to quantify.

With the US economy starving for labor, the government's largest single program induces workers with productive years remaining to retire early, which most have done with alacrity.

Washington has been polarized and paralyzed in dealing with Social Security since Reagan engineered a rescue in 1983. America's twenty-first-century presidents have treated Social Security's deepening problems with malign neglect. Bush 43 proposed a partial privatization that had no hope of garnering opposition support. By the time he suggested compromise, Democrats were loath to surrender their partisan win. (Pelosi in 2005: "Why should we put a plan out? Our plan is to stop [Bush]. He must be stopped.") Shortly before his inauguration, Obama pledged to stop "kick[ing] this can down the road" and make the hard decisions regarding Social Security.[37] He created the Simpson-Bowles commission on fiscal responsibility. Its report carefully explained Social Security's aging baby boomer problem, warning darkly that "unless we act, these immense demographic changes will bring the Social Security program to its knees." Obama failed to act, and the results have indeed been dire.

Since then, Social Security has been entirely off the table. Trump repeatedly vowed not to touch the program and never advanced any reform. Biden adopted the Sanders pour-gaso-line-on-the-fire position that Social Security should *expand* by increasing benefits and categorically rejecting means testing or any other form of cost savings. This has effectively killed any serious reform prospects during his administration.

Four decades of inaction on Social Security as the largest generation in the nation's history began collecting benefits proved to be incredibly costly, just as the program's trustees and Simpson-Bowles had warned. The present value of the retirement program's actuarial shortfall grew to over $20 trillion, a figure that rivals the national debt. These choices to sit by and leave Social Security's unsound finances to successors while a well-understood situation deteriorated in plain sight was presidential neglect and malfeasance of a high order.

As with growth of the debt, millennials will suffer the most. The essence of Social Security is a vast monthly extraction of money from the working young and payment to the retired old. In the past, with productivity and incomes rising fast, this could be justified as an inter-generational transfer from the future-rich youth to the present-poor elderly. Now, with millennials lagging behind their parents on all key financial measures, the nation's most expensive program has morphed from Robin Hood into the sheriff of Nottingham.

Voter self-interest makes this kind of preference for older citizens less surprising. Every voter is already old or plans to be, while none will be young again, creating a systemic bias favoring the elderly. But circumstances changed when transfer payments became the federal government's principal budgetary function. America now risks becoming a gerontocracy—government of, by, and for the elderly. It seems no coincidence that the 2020 presidential candidates were by far the oldest in history, breaking the record set in 2016. The parties' likely 2024 nominees hardly suggest an impending youth movement.

Whether by design or happenstance, millennials must pay more into Social Security than they will ever get out; no other result remains possible. Neglect of the problem while retiring baby boomers collected trillions of dollars in early-retirement benefits has foreclosed any win-win outcomes that might have existed earlier. That money is not coming back.

The goal of the next president must therefore be to (1) subordinate partisan considerations and (2) move immediately to limit the damage to America's future while (3) preserving Social Security's essential function of providing financial security for the nation's elderly and (4) respecting some modicum of generational equity. Sensible approaches might include the following:

Phasing out the early-retirement option. When Franklin Roosevelt fixed the Social Security retirement age at 65, the life expectancy was 64. Now, with Americans living fifteen years longer and beginning benefits three years earlier, with the fertility rate dropping by nearly half, the payer-to-payee ratio has become unsustainably low.

This simple arithmetic is too rarely performed, perhaps because voters can easily understand it. Assume sixty years from the first paycheck to the last Social Security check. Even with forty years of nonstop full-time employment, a nearly optimal example, Social Security contributions fall well short of covering twenty years of monthly retirement checks (plus spousal and prior spousal benefits). Social Security was never meant to support so many for so long, and the deteriorating demographics caused by the baby boom and bust have made that altogether untenable.

But forty-five years of contributions just might cover fifteen years of checks. Phasing out early retirement (subject to a hardship proviso for people with life-shortening conditions) could come close to achieving that result. Most Americans in their early to middle 60s are fully capable of supporting themselves, even if they have lost a step. Social Security is simply underwriting their choice to retire early and enjoy more years of leisure subsidized by their working children, exactly the opposite of what their aging nation needs from them. Given the absence of any real hardship, the phaseout period should be compressed, initiating the first round of changes quickly.

Means testing. The federal government takes money from current workers to send Warren Buffett his monthly Social Security check. Mr. Buffett would never ask the next guy in line to pay for his Big Mac and Coke just because he is old. Of course, he *earned* a retirement check, and he does not *deserve* to be deprived of it, but neither do present and future taxpayers *deserve* the burden of enriching the wealthy when they will never see such generous benefits themselves.

When decades of Americans have collected far more than they contributed, someone must be on the losing end to balance that equation. The essential questions become less right and wrong and more damage control: Who can better absorb the unfair hit, and what allocation of that burden will best serve the nation? To date, the decision has been to cover present recipients in full and burden younger American workers with all the cost, regardless of their relative means. Taking financial situations into account must be less unfair than that. Phasing out retirement benefits beginning only at higher income levels (e.g., above $150,000 per year before Social Security) would still produce considerable savings.

Limited means testing would focus Social Security on its core social insurance purpose while shrinking the poor-youth-to-rich-elderly transfers. Congress could initiate this change on a modest scale with little delay. Shortchanging solidly affluent retirees—triggering at most minor lifestyle adjustments or slight reductions of their heirs' prospects—is hardly the kind of sacrifice that requires long preparation.

Reducing cost of living adjustments. The simplest approach is rarely considered—just reduce future after-tax payouts to partially offset the effect of longer life spans and accommodate fiscal reality, with a phase-in period adequate to allow workers to increase their retirement savings or plan to work a year or two longer. Social Security is so large that even tinkering at the margins could yield real savings. The record-breaking 2021 and 2022 cost of living adjustments were body blows for a program that was already staggering, with monthly checks increasing faster than payroll contributions. Simpson-Bowles suggested substituting a chain-weighted for fixed-weight consumer price index[38] for a more accurate reflection of retirees' true cost of living changes. Just taxing 100 percent rather than 80 percent of Social Security payments to beneficiaries with incomes over $100,000 would yield more than $5 billion annually, with no detectable effect on those taxpayers' lifestyles.

Congress has increased entitlement benefits many times, just because the money was there. No commandment prohibits a change in the opposite direction after that money is gone, helping to restore Social Security's solvency and alleviate the lifetime burden on millennials.

These and other alternatives deserve detailed study and refinement. The point here is that reform sooner is better than crisis later, but it will happen only if some 2024 presidential candidate shows the courage to inject this "third rail" issue into the public conversation.

Despite all the passionate denials and political posturing, Washington must cut Social Security outlays or increase contributions substantially. It is unthinkable to borrow trillions more dollars shoring up unsustainable benefits, paid to older Americans who could easily do with less by younger Americans who can't, or it should be. A presidential candidate proposing commonsense changes to restore Social Security's finances while protecting its vulnerable beneficiaries might earn a surprising amount of independent and moderate support for finally facing up to reality with the voters.

Crime

Through America's rising prosperity and global ascendance in the 1980s, one national embarrassment stood out—high crime rates. The homicide rate, fueled in part by the violence--soaked crack cocaine trade in inner cities, remained near record highs, multiple times those in Europe or Japan.

In 1994 President Clinton signed the largest omnibus crime bill in US history. It had passed in both houses with strong majorities from both parties, the last major federal anticrime law passed with substantial bipartisan support. It included a program called Community Oriented Policing Services (COPS) to provide grants that would enable states and cities to hire new officers for expanded community policing. Largely due to COPS, over eighty thousand new officers were hired between 1994 and 1998 and mostly deployed to beats in higher crime areas.

This legislation failed to impress the nation's leading criminologists, who had already concluded that police kept order in the streets but had little impact on crime rates. In 1995 and 1996 alone, James Q. Wilson, James Fox, and John DiIulio independently forecast new peaks in violent--crime figures based on adverse demographic trends, essentially discounting any favorable impact from additional cops on the street. They could not have been more wrong had they tried. The carnage in America's cities was already in decline, with COPS playing an important role.

Results varied among cities, with New York City as the clear leader. New York had essentially the same violent-crime statistics as other large American cities in 1993. All those cities improved, but New York improved about twice as much on every measure. Murders, for example, fell by 75 percent, from 2,420 in 1993 to 616 in 2014,[39] even as the population rose. The poor city dweller in 2014 had about the same chance of being victimized by crime as the affluent resident of 1993,[40] a quality of life sea change in lower-income areas. As early as 2000, New York had the lowest serious crime rates of any large American city in almost every category, and it continued to improve. Berkeley law professor Franklin Zimring, a veteran criminal justice expert not given to gushing, described this as "a reversal in crime and violence beyond the imagination of responsible policy analysts . . . achieved without any fundamental change in the population composition, economy, or ecology of New York City."[41] It is therefore the city that criminologists study for what worked best.

The first factor requires little discussion—more police. Leveraging funds available from COPS, full-time NYPD employees rose by a third, which was more than the increases in other major cities. Because the funds were earmarked for community policing, most of those new officers were beat cops, although, importantly, the detective roster also lengthened. A steadier and more visible presence in high crime and marginal areas discouraged some of the open and obvious criminal activities, like sidewalk and drive-by crack sales. They also shortened response times, potentially preventing the escalation of a violent situation and improving the potential for gathering eyewitness evidence or even apprehending perpetrators on the spot.

The largest factor setting New York apart following COPS was the more efficient and strategic utilization of these additional officers to discourage crime and prosecute offenders. This was enabled by a management system called CompStat (computerized statistics), the brainchild of Jack Maple and William Bratton, transit police who became thought leaders of NYPD at the critical moment of 1994.[42] They built it on four policing principles: accurate, timely intelligence; rapid deployment; effective tactics; and relentless follow-up. Highly detailed crime data began to be compiled daily to identify any patterns, new or distinctive modi operandi, possible perpetrators, other precincts with related events, and so on. Precinct captains appeared monthly before the CompStat panel for intensive real-time or postmortem critiques, brainstorming, resource reallocations, and accountability. It was a programmatic and information-based attempt to systematize criminal investigation, to concentrate resources where they would deliver the greatest value, and to summon the knowledge of the whole department against every perpetrator, gang, and criminal organization—in short, to make the contest between criminals and police as unfair as possible—the antithesis of the mano a mano matchups dramatized in *Kojak* or *NYPD Blue*.

More police plus the CompStat process worked. Homicide, robbery, and other violent-crime arrest rates began rising almost immediately.[43] This simultaneously furthered two goals: incapacitation (taking hardened criminals off the streets) and deterrence (persuading less hardened criminals that crime doesn't pay). The incidence of those crimes fell substantially within three years, then continued falling at a lesser rate. Mayors Giuliani and Bloomberg were strong supporters throughout, a rare point of concurrence between them. New York City's contributions to state prison populations initially rose but then flattened and declined, suggesting that some regular offenders quit offending or moved elsewhere. Dozens of other large cities soon adopted CompStat and its variants, which continued to produce positive results.

From 1994 to 2014, the United States experienced the largest decline in serious crime in its history. Overall, violent crime fell by about half, with most of the gains concentrated in the first six years. The depth, breadth, and durability of these declines startled even the most sanguine observers. The US ceased to be an outlier in international crime comparisons. Multiple factors contributed, but COPS mattered.

Regrettably but predictably, this lasting success bred complacency. With crime so diminished, anticrime programs began to feel like fighting the last war. The public felt secure. Pew Research tracks voters' top concerns in advance of each presidential election. By 2004 crime had disappeared from the list, not to return until riot-torn 2020. Objections to overly intrusive policing and high rates of imprisonment gained traction. The US prison population declined by 128,000 (8 percent) from 2014 to 2019.

Other budget priorities took precedence. COPS funding for community policing fell sharply. Full-time law enforcement officers peaked at 709,000 (2.4 per thousand population) in 2008 before falling to a low point of 628,000 (2.0 per thousand) in 2014. Police were being partially defunded.

Not surprisingly, crime rates turned upward. The change began gradually; then homicides spiked by 30 percent in 2020, the largest one-year increase in the nation's history, and remained high. To date, this spike has been concentrated in a few dozen hotspots. Two cities tell the tale.

Chicago has been prone to violent-crime problems going back to Prohibition, but the current surge is beyond the pale. Homicides rose from five hundred in 2019 to eight hundred in 2021, a 60 percent increase in two years. These fatalities exceed eighteen per hundred thousand population, five times the per capita homicide rate of New York City. Boeing and Caterpillar relocated their corporate headquarters out of Chicago largely to escape this wave of violence. The killings are heavily concentrated in a relative handful of neighborhoods, some of which had over one hundred homicides per hundred thousand population. Gang activity was a major cause. Ever fewer police are available to confront this rising tide, as retirements and resignations have far outnumbered new academy gradu-ates in recent years.

The City of Brotherly Love is not living up to its name. Philadelphia's homicide rate per capita broke its prior record in 2021. At thirty-five homicides per hundred thousand residents, it nearly doubled Chicago's grim figure, with no apparent improvement in 2022. The police clear fewer than half of these killings and only about 20 percent of nonfatal shootings. A deputy commissioner of police expressed abject resignation: "If we don't have a video to show exactly what happened, . . . we are having a hard time clearing that case."[44] The police department of the sixth-largest city in the nation apparently lacks the wherewithal to actually solve a murder not recorded for posterity. As in Chicago, Philadelphia's police are badly understaffed. They are already 20 percent short of their full complement, with scheduled future retirements outnumbering potential academy graduates. This limits street presence, lengthens response times, and all but precludes the kinds of follow-up investigation that often close cases. Philadelphia's district attorney campaigned on reducing the prison population, had a history of suing the police department, and has been weak on prosecuting felony suspects when police manage to arrest them. Morale is low, sapping initiative.

Chicago and Philadelphia are only the largest cities experiencing this surge. Atlanta, New Orleans, and Portland have suffered through even steeper spikes in homicides. They have many vacancies in their police forces and low closure rates.

This problem will likely expand. Nationwide, police have become targets of violence. A record number were shot in the line of duty in 2021, some in premeditated ambushes rather than spur-of-the-moment confrontations. Police having to watch their backs lose their focus.

Recruitment is harder, and some veteran officers are deciding to take their pensions while they still can. Full-time law enforcement officers declined by thirty-six thousand in 2021, and that decline extended into 2022. Affirmative measures will be needed to stem this exodus and attract new applicants to law enforcement careers.

COPS redux is a solution with a proved track record, with only partisanship standing in the way. To date, Progressive Caucus members who had urged defunding the police in 2020 have blocked congressional passage of any federal grant program to put more cops on the street. The administration, so active in pushing for more spending, new entitlements, and climate change initiatives, has invested no capital in breaking through its own party's resistance. Republicans who felt no urge to hand Biden an accomplishment before the midterms were all too happy to stand by and see Democrats hoisted by their own petard. Partisan paralysis in the face of this crime spike is a tangible disservice to the nation. Mounting evidence shows that, although America does not need a police state, it badly needs police.

The frequent mass shootings of recent years call out for some limited gun control, but common ground has proved hard to find. Polls show broad public support for three restrictions on gun sales: background checks on all purchasers; prohibiting sales to persons convicted of domestic violence crimes and the mentally ill; and a minimum age of twenty-one.[45] Any such restrictions must pass constitutional muster, but applying the same age limit for purchasing a deadly weapon as for a shot of whiskey hardly suggests a slippery slope toward repealing the Second Amendment. Although these restrictions would not broadly cure the nation's violent-crime rate, preventing even a few slaughters is worth the trouble.

Criminal fatalities do not always entail violence. The CDC estimates seventy-one thousand deaths from accidental fentanyl overdose in 2021, mostly young adults and teens, with further increases almost certain in 2022. This death toll is more than *triple* the number of homicides and double that of any other street drug. Fentanyl-meth drug combinations also kill tens of thousands of Americans annually, and rising.

Mexican cartels import the raw materials from China, compound low-grade fentanyl in bulk, then smuggle it into the US by the ton for further refinement or compounding and distribution. Even with drug dealer markups, fentanyl is inexpensive compared to crystal meth or heroin; a teen can buy a fatal dose with pocket money. Paralleling crack cocaine in the late 1980s, fentanyl has become a public health menace. Statistically, its importation and sale are the deadliest crimes in America. A president making this a priority could use diplomatic pressure on China and Mexico to discourage their tacit collusion in this trade, better interdiction at the border, and focused Drug Enforcement Administration enforcement efforts to curtail this epidemic.

Voters rank crime prevention as one of the top issues facing the nation. They will support a presidential candidate who rejects the ideologies of both sides, bringing moderates together to restore and preserve order and safety on the streets and protect the nation's youth.

Election Reform

A division of the republic into two great parties . . .
concerting measures in opposition to each other . . .
is to be dreaded as the greatest public evil.
—John Adams, 1789

The Constitution never mentions political parties, and George Washington loathed and despised them. They are a necessary evil in the modern world; eliminating them would be neither possible nor desirable. Still, party allegiance can never be allowed to supersede or undermine the more noble allegiance to the nation's ideals and founding principles. Nothing restricts lawmakers or the voters themselves from trimming the parties' power when, as now, they overreach their authority to the detriment of the common good.

America needs at least one mainstream presidential candidate in the 2024 general election who is qualified and suitable for the Oval Office, but that is only a start toward reversing excessive partisanship. In the longer term, the nation must adopt election procedures that *routinely* produce such candidates, as they did prior to this century, without the need for exceptional, extra-party efforts of organizations like No Labels (see Chapter Three below). Current elections are miserably failing that test. Partisans' undue influence in the primaries is the principal culprit.

The nation's largest group of voters is also its least influential. Registered independents now outnumber either Republicans or Democrats by roughly 30 percent nationwide, the result of waning allegiance to the major parties as they have become more polarizing. With independents' share highest among younger voters and lowest among older voters, time is the independents' friend— their plurality should only expand and might reach an absolute majority. Yet both parties dismiss their more centrist and pragmatic views as a mere nuisance, peripheral if not irrelevant to the election-year scorched earth wars waged between right- and left-wingers. This produces government of the extremes, by the extremes, and for the extremes, a perversion of Lincoln's vision. Independents' views better reflect the nation's mainstream and therefore deserve the most attention, not the least. Ignoring them is the antithesis of democratic principles.

Independents could and should become more diligent in making their voices heard, but many existing election laws and practices are stacked against them, encouraging a sense of exclusion and futility. In 2016 and 2020, the vote that mattered most was in the primaries, because both parties' presidential nominees were unacceptable to most mainstream voters, and it was too late for a challenger to emerge. This consigned tens of millions of voters, especially independents, to casting nega-votes or skipping the presidential election altogether.

It is thus vital to participate in the primaries to have any meaningful say in America's governance, but about half the states have closed primaries—that is, primaries reserved to parties and party members. The parties' extremism drove out independents and moderates; then party-supported laws prevent or discourage them from voting in the primaries, denying them any practical involvement in selecting their president. This bears repeating. *Parties ceased to represent the interests of moderate party members, causing millions of them to leave those parties; then party politicians limited their political participation outside the parties.* This systematic disenfranchisement of independents has become a self-reinforcing failure of American democracy. Denying or restricting independents' access to the primaries has strongly favored fringe candidates in recent election cycles. The damaging results have become painfully clear.

Apart from these legal impediments, the primary turnout is unrepresentative ideologically and often too low to be statistically meaningful. The 2016 presidential primaries vividly illustrate both problems. Senator Sanders received nearly as many votes as Secretary Clinton, although comparatively few Democrats shared his socialist views. Donald Trump and Senator Ted Cruz, the two largest primary vote getters, were nowhere near the ideological center of Republican voters.

Partisans on both sides also exploit the primaries' low and unrepresentative turnout to polarize Congress. In 2014 House Majority Leader Eric Cantor (R) lost his seat to a primary challenge by a largely unknown Tea Party candidate. Cantor was popular in his district, with a scandal-free record, and his high leadership position helped his constituents. Few Republicans in his Virginia district were Tea Partiers, but the tiny primary electorate voted that way. In 2018 AOC, a little-known 29-year-old activist working as a waitress and bartender, ousted ten-term Congressman Joe Crowley in the primary election for New York's fourteenth congressional district, a safe Democratic seat. A mainstream Democrat, Crowley had the endorsements of Senators Schumer and Kirsten Gillibrand and New York City Mayor Bill de Blasio. AOC gathered just 17,000 votes in a district with a population of 750,000, but it was enough to carry a midterm primary. She would have stood little or no chance against Crowley in any election with statistically meaningful numbers of voters.

Results like these show how vulnerable incumbents may be to primary challengers, and that vulnerability provides the fringes with leverage. "Primary" has become a transitive verb roughly synonymous with "threaten"— extremists may decide to "primary" any incumbent found lacking in ideological purity.[46] Senator Kyrsten Sinema faced a probable primary challenge in 2024 for her refusal to repeal the filibuster. Left-wing activists viewed her as a turncoat for not silencing her fifty Republican colleagues when she had the chance, clouding her prospects for renomination (now rendered moot by her registration as an independent). If primary electorates remain small and unrepresentative, they could become the death knell for moderate legislators.

The 2022 election revived another unsavory primary trick promoting fringe candidates: the fake cross-party primary endorsement. Democratic candidates and their financial backers spent $50 million on television spots supporting right-wing election deniers in thirteen state primary races, even as their party leaders (properly) condemned election denial for undermining trust in the democratic process.[47] Six of those candidates won their primaries, enabling them to continue spreading their divisive story for two additional months before losing in the general election. From a purely partisan standpoint, the trick worked admirably, producing six Democratic winners in otherwise iffy contests.

At least one of these had national implications. In New Hampshire the Democrats' Senate Majority PAC spent $3 million attacking moderate Chuck Morse (endorsed by Governor Chris Sununu), helping to lift adamant election denier Don Bolduc to a one-point victory in the Republican primary.[48] Moderate Democratic incumbent Maggie Hassan easily defeated Bolduc in the general election, where Morse would have been favored to win. A flip of the New Hampshire Senate seat would have denied Democrats control of the Senate.

This was extreme partisan excess, which the Biden administration pointedly refused to condemn. It is rank hypocrisy to win by publicly supporting politicians and positions you abhor. Voters are entitled to choose between the parties' strongest candidates. Beyond the matter of principle, however, two can play at this game. Given its success for Democrats, Republicans may copy this tactic in 2024 by airing ads in support of "defund the police" or open-border extremists in Democratic primaries. The net result would be even fewer moderate candidates on both sides and more general election contests between broadly disliked political outliers.

The need for expanding primary election participation is widely acknowledged. Many reform-minded organizations are actively pursuing those goals in state legislatures and through ballot initiatives. Such reform is fundamental and essential, but it need not be a *precondition* of giving mainstream views a stronger voice in Washington. Extremists benefit from the existing rules and practices, while centrists suffer from them. A victory or even a strong showing by a centrist or moderate presidential candidate, regardless of party affiliation, could only provide momentum for antipartisan primary reforms. Presidents do not make state election laws, but they can and should set a tone by encouraging more inclusion of independents and broader participation in primaries.

Partisanship and Polarization

We must not seek to defeat or humiliate the enemy but to win his friendship and understanding.
—Martin Luther King Jr., 1957

One trait uniquely characterizes twenty-first-century Washington: polarization. Both parties have mastered the rhetoric of self-righteousness and vilification at the expense of fairness, decency, and cooperation. They have too often exalted partisanship over citizenship or confused the two. Politicians treat opposing-party members like enemies of the state rather than fellow Americans who need persuading. Both sides rely primarily on fearmongering campaigns. While that continues, effective governance stands little chance.

This extreme political climate has overflowed into broader society and everyday life. The shared sense of community has declined. Americans increasingly choose their states, their neighborhoods, their social lives, and their friends based on political compatibility. The choice of news and information sources too often becomes a definitive pledge of allegiance. Belief and preference imperceptibly morph into dogmatic assertions. Deference and mutual respect have waned. Inconvenient facts disappear into the memory hole, never to be acknowledged or credited. Disagreement too often ends in anger, dismissal, and contempt. It becomes harder and rarer to set aside political differences even in ordinary social and civic dealings.

The president of the United States has a unique role in restoring and maintaining bipartisanship and civility. That august title deserves a careful reading: the occupant of the Oval Office is the singular officeholder who was elected by *all American voters* to lead, represent, and serve *the entire nation*, domestically and internationally. It is an awesome responsibility, which recent presidents have failed to meet, despite their campaign commitments to the contrary.

In his acceptance speech at the Republican Party's 2000 convention, George Bush pledged to be "a uniter, not a divider," decrying "the bitter arguments of the last few years."[49] His promise sounded plausible. He had governed Texas with a Democratic legislature and stayed aloof from the impeachment of President Clinton, who had become friendly with his father. His campaign denounced partisan bickering, and his "compassionate conservatism" campaign slogan sounded inclusive, but the selection of Dick Cheney as his running mate was a bad omen. The former secretary of defense was known for his intellect and energy but also for his hard-edged neoconservative ideology, sharp tongue, sharper elbows, and appetite for partisan conflict: an odd fit with a campaign predicated on bipartisanship. The vice president's polarizing influence would be felt throughout the Bush administration.[50]

Like Governor Bush, Senator Obama committed to "turn the page on the ugly partisanship in Washington so we can bring Democrats and Republicans together to pass an agenda." "I don't want to pit Red America against Blue America." This rhetoric appealed to disillusioned voters, but it also proved empty. An early portent was the choice of Rahm Emanuel as chief of staff, the second most important position in the White House. Nicknamed Rahmbo, Emanuel was legendary for his ferociously partisan take-no-prisoners approach that quickly categorized people as assets or enemies and proceeded accordingly. His default attitude was fury; his most common motive, revenge. From the moment of his appointment, few Republicans trusted the president-elect's professions of bipartisanship, and the reality too rarely belied their expectations. Obama may have hoped for change, but he deepened divisions between the parties.[51] By 2012 even the soothing rhetoric had disappeared, as a disillusioned president waged a negative partisan campaign, vilifying Mitt Romney and appealing only to his base.

As Congress became ever more divided and mean spirited, the nation needed a unifying presence in the White

House. It got the opposite. The two presidents who campaigned most fervently on reducing partisanship became deeply polarizing leaders in office, setting the stage for the triumphs of extremism in the 2016 and 2020 elections.

Donald Trump rarely pretended and never intended to be a healer. He was openly adversarial, divisive, and proud of it. He laced his campaign speeches with anger, derision, and mockery. He threatened to name a special prosecutor to investigate Hillary Clinton. Jailing one's defeated opponents is a hallmark of autocracy, not democracy. Time and again, he confused loyalty to him with loyalty to America.

In office, insults were Trump's go-to response to political opposition. President Obama: "the most ignorant President in our history"; "perhaps the worst President in American history"; "a bad (or sick) guy" who "had my wires tapped." Senator Schumer: "a clown." Mark Cuban: "not smart enough to run for President." CBS and NBC News: "enemy of the American people." *New York Times*: "a joke." Senator Sanders: "crazy." Senator Romney: "a fool." John Bolton: "one of the dumbest people in Washington." Back on the campaign trail in 2020, he called Vice President Biden "the candidate of rioters, looters, arsonists, gun-grabbers, flag-burners, and Marxists," "wacko," "low IQ," "corrupt," and "criminal." If reelected in 2024, Trump has promised to grant full pardons to rioters convicted of violent crimes committed in the Capitol building with Congress in session, because they supported him. A more abrasive and less suitable temperament in the Oval Office would be hard to imagine.

Candidate Biden mostly projected moderation, but President Biden immediately made common cause with Senator Sanders and Democrats' progressive left wing, trying to remake America on a party line basis. This was a clear repudiation of anything that Republicans or moderate independents could support. That "worked" with party line passage of the COVID stimulus bill, which spurred inflation, just as Larry Summers had said it would.[52] Biden spent the remainder of 2021 promoting the highly partisan BBB bill. In 2022, with his popularity at record lows and the midterms looming, Biden pulled another line item from the Progressive Caucus agenda, forgiving $426 billion of student loan debt. Knowing this would be defeated in the Senate on fiscal and fairness grounds, he used an executive order, the most partisan and least democratic tool at his disposal, despite his later claims that he had gotten it "passed" as a "law." The courts are deciding whether this was unconstitutional, but it was undeniably partisan and polarizing. The internal administration debate, if any, was just that; there is no record of any discussions with legislators about the president's intentions.

Each of these presidents took office in a dysfunctional capital, and each made it more so. Contrast this with the records of twentieth-century presidents who worked with their political opponents to achieve great things for the nation. At the signing of the Civil Rights Act of 1964, Johnson handed the first signature pen to his longtime adversary Senator Dirksen. Speaker Tip O'Neill and other prominent Democrats called to congratulate Reagan on the passage of tax cuts that O'Neill had resisted strenuously. Clinton and Gingrich, never buddies, worked closely together for five productive years, the like of which have not been seen since. Each of these unlikely duos proved that politics need not be a zero-sum game.

Often, presidents compromised even when they might have prevailed without it, gaining broader support and preserving the law when the next election went against them. Moderate leaders may be more than willing to compromise instead of going for the kill.[53] Aside from simple decency, this can be savvy politics. Long experience shows that *half a loaf may be better than the whole loaf*. Some unsuspected wisdom or value often lurks in the opposition position—elections confer power and too often cockiness, but never infallibility. Negotiated results may also be less vulnerable to sabotage. When one side gets all it wants, the other loses nothing by ruining that loaf when given the chance. Pious recriminations do not alter this regrettable fact of human nature.

Partisan Congresses must share the blame for Washington's chronic dysfunctionality, but the buck stops in the Oval Office. It is ultimately the president's job to represent all Americans, to be the grown-up in the room, and to achieve durable, bipartisan progress rather than heightening tensions for short-term gain, however well intentioned. America's recent presidents have failed in this respect, and that failure has had more profound and lasting consequences than any of their transitory successes.

Americans consistently express a strong preference for bipartisan legislating and policy making in Washington. A moderate or centrist candidate dedicated to some purpose higher than enhancing partisan advantage, who favored negotiation and compromise to resolve differences, would tap into a potent source of voter support.

Polarized Washington, led or at least abetted by the partisans in chief, has ignored or mishandled these and other important issues for too long. Invoking the shade of President Reagan, Americans need to ask whether we are better or worse off compared to 2016. For readers who still harbor doubts, a few lowlights should quiet them.

SUBJECT	2016-23 COMPARISON
ECONOMY	Worse. The economy has experienced little real, sustained growth over six years, with one recession in 2020 and another likely in 2023. Millennials' standard of living lags significantly behind their parents' on almost every measure. America's global economic standing continues to erode.
INFLATION	Incomparably worse. Inflation had been quelled since 1983. Severe interest rate increases barely kept inflation in single digits in 2022. Wage increases cannot keep pace. Many negative repercussions from the inflation surge and the curative measures remain to be felt.
DEBT	Much worse. Deficits were historically high from 2003–16, but those now pale compared to the flood of red ink experienced since, taking the nation's debt to the highest and most dangerous level in its history with no justification or lasting benefits from this reckless fiscal experiment.

GLOBAL STANDING	Much worse. No region of the world is more stable or more supportive of America than in 2016. The dictatorial powers of China and Russia have been setting the global agenda. America's partisan foreign policy approach has been tried and found wanting.
CLIMATE CHANGE	Worse. Dashing the hopes engendered by Paris and *Energiewende*, global carbon emissions have risen to record levels, shattering every projection. The Intergovernmental Panel on Climate Change's previous 2030 and 2050 emission goals are dead letters despite huge expenditures. The Paris global diplomacy/shared pain approach has been tested to destruction.
IMMIGRATION	Much worse. America has accomplished the worst possible outcome—too few legal immigrant workers and families and too many illegals—with no end in sight. Drug trafficking is up sharply. Portions of the southern border are in crisis.

SOCIAL SECURITY	**Much worse. The nation's largest program is six years closer to insolvency. Nothing has been done. The options that remain will be painful.**
CRIME	**Much worse. Violent-crime rates that fell by half from 1991 to 2014 have since jumped sharply, with homicides up over 30 percent from 2018 to 2022.**
POLARIZATION	**Much worse. President Trump insults and attacks President Biden and his voters, and vice versa. The ideals of civility and respectful disagreement are not merely flouted in Washington, they are openly ridiculed.**

The blame is widely shared, but one glaring cause predominates. Americans have unavoidably elected bad presidents because the major parties nominated the wrong candidates. Voters need to address this problem at its root by demanding a real choice in the 2024 general election. Chapter Three describes how.

CHAPTER THREE

THE SOLUTION

Mere passive citizenship is not enough. Men must be aggressive for what is right if government is to be saved from men who are aggressive for what is wrong.
—Robert LaFollette, 1924

We are called to be architects of the future, not its victims.
—Buckminster Fuller

C hapter One described America's steeply declining quality of governance, driven by a self-reinforcing cycle of polarization. The parties' systemic inability to nominate suitable presidential candidates has been a major contributor to this decline. Serious observers acknowledge that reality, whatever their political leanings, but too many then fight over assigning the blame instead of trying to agree on a cure.

Chapter Two described examples of what a return to more bipartisan governance might accomplish. In a less polarized Washington, discussion, negotiation, and compromise could begin to resolve problems that have proved intractable in the existing toxic atmosphere.

Chapter Three addresses how voters may be able to confront and solve this national crisis, seemingly against all odds. The major parties enjoy duopoly power over politics in the US, and their extremist wings are firmly in control at a national level, but those partisans lack broad popular support. Washington has become government of the *parties*. Most Americans reject leadership by Trump loyalists or by the progressive left. They remember being proud of their presidents and want that feeling again.

Mainstream voters are deeply dissatisfied with Washington's reckless economic, budgetary, environmental, social, and foreign policy follies, with large majorities seeing America as fundamentally on the wrong track. Senator Sinema's post-midterm registration as an independent suggests that some highly placed elected officials may share voters' dissatisfaction. "There's a disconnect between what everyday Americans want and deserve from our politics, and what political parties are offering," Sinema wrote in an editorial announcing the change. "Bipartisan compromise is seen as a rarely acceptable last resort, rather than the best way to achieve lasting progress. Payback against the opposition party has replaced thoughtful legislating."[1]

How many other prominent political figures might be prepared to brave the wrath of their ideological colleagues and support bipartisan progress, if only the climate in Washington became more conducive? A more opportune time than 2024 would be hard to imagine.

But a conducive climate still needs ways and means to effect change. A sensible centrist political core needs renewed focus and novel mechanisms to overcome the partisan biases of the primaries and restore its grasp on the levers of power. If that majority has the will to regain control of the White House, the means exist.

The nation needs a president worthy of the office. Voters must be offered at least one candidate to vote *for* rather than *against* before that experience fades into history. The polarized presidential primaries are the choke point. Only two viable solutions exist: (1) expanding voter participation in primaries to produce major party nominees who better represent mainstream America or (2) bypassing the primary process altogether with an independent candidacy. The common thread is re-empowerment of millions of Americans who feel abandoned or repelled by the divergence of the major parties.

This chapter briefly outlines the problems, the opportunities, and the challenges of each approach.

Winning a Nomination

Primaries heavily favor fringe candidates of both parties, as described above. Organizations including Unite America, OpenPrimaries, and No Labels have rallied behind open primaries and related reforms to lessen that bias, with some success. At a minimum such reforms allow independents to cast a ballot in either party's presidential primary. More ambitious initiatives, like the recent Alaska election-law overhaul and Final Five voting, seek to provide moderate candidates a pathway to victory in the general election. These efforts have intensified since the 2016 and 2020 election cycles highlighted the dangers of the existing rules, but they usually meet vigorous or passive resistance at the state level from both major parties (perhaps their only point of agreement), which are eager to preserve their control over the political process. This reform effort will therefore take time. Too little will change quickly enough to alter the trajectory of the 2024 presidential nomination process.

This primary bias presents a formidable obstacle, but it could be overcome by a concerted effort. Many more independents must participate to give moderate candidates a fair chance of nomination. Independents are already eligible to vote in roughly half the states' presidential primaries, even if it requires an extra effort. In the other states, a major party candidate worthy of the White House should also be worth temporarily declaring a major party affiliation for the sole purpose of participating in the primaries, before re-registering as an independent.

Major party voters have no excuse—they need only cast a primary ballot. Polls show that both parties' voters want change. *Until the political fringes lose their primary choke holds, electing the right president will require those voters to cast two votes rather than one.* One more vote every four years is a modest burden to bear for democracy. Millions more Americans must embrace primary voting as a privilege, a duty, and an opportunity of citizenship.

Well-known get-out-the-vote methods, routinely employed in general elections, would expand primary voter turnout. It just takes individuals, organizations, employers, donors, and media to recognize the need and pitch in. None of this is easy, but it is straightforward and executable.

Higher turnout is necessary but not sufficient. Mainstream voters need to approach early primaries strategically, concentrating their votes in support of the moderate with the best chance of winning the nomination and the general election. One moderate has a chance, despite the primaries' bias. Spreading the moderate vote among multiple candidates just paves the way for the fringes to prevail with their committed minority support.

In any choice between *moderation* and *party*, moderation is what the nation needs. The United States cannot regain its identity or the path of progress without cooperation in solving the nation's problems. But moderation versus party may be a false dichotomy. The major party that nominates a moderate to oppose an extremist candidate of the other, in either direction, will enjoy at least one large advantage in the general election—a natural appeal to independent voters. The base strategy would have little chance against this inreach toward the center in the current environment. That neither party has chosen to seize this advantage in recent elections is a mark of extremists' all-or-nothing attitude and their death grip over party processes.

This strategy would require a sharp departure from recent history. Trump followers and progressive leftists have dominated the primaries, most recently in 2020 and 2022. In state after state, nominees poorly reflected the electorate's views. Moderate politicians must perceive a real chance of prevailing if they are to brave the vitriol of their extremist wings, risking political futures inside their parties built over their lifetimes. But political courage has emerged before in times of need, and it may be doing so again: witness the principled stands of Vice President Pence, Senators Manchin and Sinema, and Congresswoman Liz Cheney, regardless of personal sacrifice.

Trump's early declaration of his 2024 candidacy reduced the chances for a viable moderate Republican candidate. Trump commands only minority support, but that minority votes in primaries. Denying him the nomination would be challenging. Late 2022 polls suggest that Florida governor Ron DeSantis might succeed, but why should he run in 2024? Even if successful, his primary candidacy could become a kamikaze mission. Trump punishes fellow Republicans' disloyalty to him personally. He might respond to losing the nomination by blowing up the party. Even half the Trumpsters skipping the general election would doom the Republican candidate. DeSantis is only 44, giving him the luxury of picking his battles. Why choose to create an influential enemy who will vanish on his own with the passage of another four years? Patience seems a promising strategy for DeSantis personally. Whether any other Republicans could unseat Trump in the primaries remains to be seen.

A criminal prosecution in Georgia or other extra-political event could derail Trump's candidacy and open the door for other Republicans with a chance of winning. Otherwise, the prospects are iffy.

The Democrats' situation depends first on Biden, who does not enjoy Trump's death grip over his party's prospects. If he seeks the nomination, any opposition will be seen as divisive, but a moderate opponent could be the Democrats' strongest option against Trump or any other extremist Republican. Biden would be saddled with his unpopularity along with age and health issues, and a leftist challenger might be viewed as continuing a failed administration. A moderate could campaign from the center as the vaccine against the Trump virus.

If Biden drops out early, a moderate would face left-wing opponents, with the Democratic primaries' liberal bias providing their tailwind. Any prospect of another Trump presidency will strongly energize progressives to obliterate this blight forever and seize the power they know they deserve. Only a disciplined and energetic surge of mainstream primary voting has much chance of matching and overcoming the passion of the party's left wing. The starting point must be to translate the diffuse displeasure that many Democrats feel toward their extremist politicians, as reflected in many polls, into recruiting and building support for one promising moderate early in the primary cycle, long before most voters are paying attention. Even in biased primaries, one strong moderate should prevail against a pack of progressives.

Anything is possible before the primaries even begin, but a moderate's path to the nomination in either party involves multiple contingencies. A backup plan is needed.

An Independent Campaign

The alternative is for a high-profile individual to bypass the biased primary process altogether and run instead as an independent in the general election. (To keep the terminology straight, a Republican or Democrat running in the general election outside party auspices becomes an "Independent" candidate for these purposes.)

The parties' recent offerings have enjoyed little public approval. The Trump and Biden administrations' unfavorable ratings have been both deep and durable. Few Americans want to see a rematch between these 2020 election contestants. This is especially true among independent voters, but millions of party members have also been disillusioned with their parties' candidates in the general elections and profess openness to an alternative.

Despite voters' dissatisfaction, a rematch, or something very similar, seems depressingly likely in 2024. Trump will be hard to oppose effectively in the Republican primaries, as described above. Biden's road to the nomination has more off-ramps, but that may not alter the situation greatly. Large percentages of voters also have "very unfavorable" impressions of the prominent progressive alternatives to Biden, including Vice President Harris; Senators Warren, Clinton, and Sanders; and Representative AOC, which often translate into nega-votes, or, at best, nonvotes. Any of those candidates would also be offering "more of the same" rather than a fresh start following the Biden administration's unpopular policies. (If a moderate Democrat were nominated, voters would already have a non-extremist choice on the ballot, so this discussion would likely become moot.)

The breadth and depth of voters' dissatisfaction translates into an unprecedented polling result: *well over half of Americans would consider a moderate or centrist Independent candidate for the presidency in 2024*, barring a surprising result in the primaries. Voters' interest in having a serious third choice cuts across party affiliation, gender, and age.[2] This interest seems durable. Polls taken in April and September 2022 produced parallel results, and the bitterness of many midterm contests only deepened the partisan divide. The percentage of voters open to supporting an independent *rose* slightly after Biden's brief surge in August 2022, suggesting a public sentiment that has taken root and has a life of its own. This presents a unique opportunity for a transformational election, a welcome ray of hope for moderates and centrists, whatever their party registration.

The only recent presidential election with broad popular interest in an independent candidate was 1992, when Ross Perot burst onto the political scene with a folksy centrist platform wrapped around a few easily grasped issues. His campaign blueprint sounds familiar three decades later. He condemned both major parties for their Washington-centricity and their detachment from the concerns of mainstream voters.[3] Large and systemic budget deficits were his central issue; he advocated budget balancing with reduced spending and targeted tax increases. He also emphasized national unity, condemning the parties' divisiveness and founding United We Stand America to encourage bipartisanship. He avoided slick and technical pitches in favor of easy-to-understand charts and commonsense voter appeals. ("I don't have any spin doctors. I don't have any speechwriters. Probably shows. I make those charts you see on TV.")

His sound bites actually bit. "I don't have any experience in running up a $4 trillion debt. I don't have any experience in gridlock government, where nobody takes any responsibility and everybody blames everybody else." "If you see a snake, just kill it. Don't appoint a committee on snakes." The budget deficit is "our legislators and our president trying to buy our votes . . . with what used to be our money. We're not that dumb." He coined "giant sucking sound" to describe the loss of manufacturing jobs overseas.

With volunteers knocking on doors, Perot quickly qualified for general election ballots. His wealth enabled him to buy extended airtime to promote his platform and further widen his name and face recognition. He briefly polled ahead of President Bush and Governor Clinton before quixotically withdrawing from the campaign, only to return to the fray in October. This withdrawal severely damaged his momentum and credibility. Despite this, he came back strongly, with polls showing he "won" the first and third presidential debates. He polled 19 percent of the popular vote, the highest non–major party showing since Theodore Roosevelt's Bull Moose campaign.

That 19 percent prompted a tectonic shift in Washington's political landscape, as the parties' survival instincts pulled both toward the center. Perot voters had coalesced into the cohesive swing vote that would decide national elections. The Republican party shifted sooner in their direction, with more visible commitment. Newt Gingrich copied Perot's platform and called it the "Contract with America" for the 1994 midterms, scrapping the Republicans' 1992 agenda, despite some vested interests' complaints. Democrats openly scoffed at this unique strategy of nationalizing midterms and touted the virtues of their single-party governance in 1993–94, a stance they soon had cause to regret. With Democratic candidates unanimously opposing the Contract and Republican candidates uniformly supporting it, the midterms boiled down to one issue and became national in character. Perot supporters broke strongly in favor of Republicans, who swept the election, earning them a House majority after four decades of uninterrupted Democratic rule. Republican House candidates received five million more votes than Democrats, a *ten million–vote swing* from the 1992 results.

It was one of the most consequential midterm elections in history. Bipartisan governance returned, with every initiative needing both Clinton's and Gingrich's approval to become law. The remaining years of the Clinton administration proved highly productive as a result, most notably with bipartisan welfare reform and budget surpluses in its last three years, a small island amid Washington's oceans of red ink, before and since.

This "Perot effect" demonstrates a vital lesson: an Independent candidate need never reside in the White House for the platform to win. *When the Independent's votes become too numerous for either major party to concede in the next election, a centripetal tug-of-war over those voters ensues.* The left and right wings either lose their influence or just lose. Perot's success forced both parties to cater to his constituency and curry his favor. Candidate Clinton had sharply criticized Perot's push for a balanced budget, arguing it would ruin the economy. President Clinton had to embrace that goal or lose the Perot voters to Republicans, and the budget was balanced on the timetable Perot had urged, while the economy grew briskly without fiscal stimulus. Ross became boss.

As in physics, the mass of those independent votes determines their gravitational pull to the center. It seems clear that any independent tally above 15 percent in 2024 would again trigger the Perot effect, transforming toxic Washington for the better.

Every indicator suggests that a quality Independent candidate could run even *stronger* than Perot in 2024. Bush and Clinton were qualified and not unpopular candidates in 1992, in sharp contrast with Biden, Trump, and their most likely replacements. Significantly, Bush was a center-right politician and Clinton was center-left, leaving a comparatively narrow centrist gap for Perot to occupy. A 2024 Independent will likely reap the benefits of a partisan chasm between the major party nominees, putting many millions of American voters in play. There will either be a weak incumbent running or none. A decisive majority of all American voters believes that the US in general and its economy in particular are on the wrong track. The nation will have suffered through two recessions plus paycheck-eating inflation in just five years, largely caused by chronic bipartisan monetary and fiscal mismanagement. Average Americans' living standards will have been flat to falling. Bad times are like manure—they stink, but they fertilize change.

The rising tide of registered independents is another favorable trend for an Independent's candidacy. Most independents lean toward one of the major parties, but even these leaners are more open to crossing lines than are party members. The shift between the 2016 and 2020 elections showed this. Biden ran much stronger than Clinton among independent voters nationwide. Exit polls showed that Biden carried Arizona, Michigan, Pennsylvania, Wisconsin, and Georgia on the strength of this shift, and those states decided the outcome. Perot won 30 percent of independent voters in 1992 (i.e., roughly even with Bush and Clinton), about double his percentage of major party voters. As the independent vote expands, an Independent's election chances improve commensurately.

A final factor favoring a 2024 Independent's candidacy is easily overlooked: many more voters now disapprove of the parties themselves than in Perot's day. Pew Research has tracked voters' party approval ratings for nearly three decades.[4] In 1994 a mere 6 percent of poll respondents viewed both parties unfavorably. That figure more than quadrupled to 27 percent in 2022. This has shrunk the party loyalist vote markedly. Rising partisanship has also intensified these negative opinions. "Very unfavorable" views, only about one-seventh of all negative responses in 1994, now constitute more than half. Very unfavorable feelings toward both parties translate into nega-votes for their nominees that an independent candidate can harvest.

Again, the views of registered independents merit special attention. Because most independents tend to vote with one party in most elections, many observers discount their supposed independence, treating them instead as "party lite." But Pew's 2022 poll reveals a shifting landscape. Nearly all leaner independents view the opposing party unfavorably, often strongly, as expected. The surprise in 2022 is that "leaners diverge from partisans in that they are far less likely to hold favorable views of the parties they lean *toward*—and those views are more negative today than they were a few years ago." Specifically, 46 percent of both leaner Democrats and leaner Republicans view their preferred parties unfavorably—they are becoming truly independent of both parties. The practical implications are clear: millions of independent voters (leaners either left or right) may enter the 2024 general election leaning *against* the party's nominee they would have been expected to favor. A centrist Independent would be the most likely beneficiary of their dissatisfaction.

Three sizable groups of voters are thus in play for an Independent presidential candidate in 2024: (1) Republicans who want to expunge the Trump legacy; (2) Democrats who object to the excessive influence of leftist elites in a party that claims to represent working Americans; and (3) independents who may find a voice in rejecting the extremism and polarization that the major parties now represent in Washington.

Given voters' growing distaste for the major parties and their likely candidates, it appears that the right independent candidate with the right support actually has a chance to win the White House in 2024, an unprecedented result in the nation's history. No Labels, an advocacy group dedicated to reducing partisanship and rancor in Washington, performed a detailed assessment based on dozens of statewide polls and concluded that an Independent "Unity Ticket" could win a plurality in twenty-three or more states, enough to carry the Electoral College. Of course, these are early days, and much may change, but even the straight-faced possibility of an Independent president marks 2024 as a unique and extraordinary opportunity for altering the status quo. Republican, Democratic, and independent moderates and centrists who can summon the will to reclaim their government from extremists have an opportunity to change the direction of this century.

Altogether, the potential for a meaningful shift in the political landscape has reached a level rarely seen in US history. If both parties adhere to their current partisan paths through this election cycle, someone outside their control might emerge to make those changes for them.

Laying the Groundwork

If not us, who? If not now, when?
—John Kennedy and Ronald Reagan (among others)

President Trump's low approval ratings and voter dissatisfaction with the left wing's dominance of the Democrats had already created an opening in the center in 2020, but no candidate materialized. Senator Amy Klobuchar was the only credible Democratic voice for bipartisanship. Despite her strong showing in New Hampshire, moderate Democrats and donors were too slow in rallying to her candidacy, and she soon dropped out of the race. Former Starbucks CEO Howard Schultz expressed an interest in running as an Independent and then withdrew. Entrepreneur and popular media figure Mark Cuban flirted with the idea but also passed. Both had received ample encouragement from independents and moderates. America was stuck with another nega-lection and another four years of national dissatisfaction, global embarrassment, and poor governance.

A better result in 2024 depends on centrists speaking out much earlier and more effectively to break the partisans' grip on presidential candidate choices.

No Labels has undertaken a bold initiative toward that end. It favors one or both parties nominating a more moderate candidate, dedicated to bipartisan governance. Failing that, however, it committed to "prequalify" an independent presidential candidate, to be named later, on the 2024 election ballots in all fifty states,[5] a novel and daunting effort. This smooths out one rough patch in any independent's road to the presidency and sends a warning to the major parties' strategists: two business-as-usual fringy candidates may face a centrist challenge. No Labels is also creating a "voter file" to help pinpoint voters who may be receptive to an independent candidacy, erasing one logistic advantage always enjoyed by the major parties, and a policy agenda built around what most Americans would like to see from Washington.

Even before the 2022 midterm elections, No Labels'

supporters had contributed tens of millions of dollars, not to elect a favorite candidate but to lay the groundwork for enabling the campaign of *some* presidential candidate deserving of that most important office and broadly acceptable to the American people. This unprecedented commitment tangibly demonstrates the breadth and depth of the nation's desire to finding a worthy occupant of the Oval Office.

But the urgency unique to an independent run for the White House extends beyond No Labels and the vital foundational steps it is taking. Any serious Independent must develop campaign assets that party candidates take for granted. The primaries generate automatic publicity for aspirants, including the debates, campaign appearances, and daily news coverage extending for months. Independents must make their own weather, arranging live events, getting interviewed, and buying airtime to get their messages out. They need to hire experienced campaign managers, produce videos, corral endorsements, set up staffs and offices, recruit volunteers, and generally prepare for ground games in all the contested states. Without party support, any serious candidate must attract over a billion dollars in donations to establish a presence comparable to that of major party candidates. (Michael Bloomberg spent that much in just four months of contending for the Democratic nomination in 2000.) That level of fund-raising without the benefit of a party apparatus requires an early start.

An Independent needs to gain recognition, credi-bility, and support from scratch, long before the general campaign begins. Major party candidates count on tens of millions of party loyalists to vote the ticket. An Inde-pendent begins with near zero votes in hand, with the daunting task of winning over each supporter.

That support must reach at least 15 percent in major nationwide polls by mid-2024, the current threshold for admission into the general election debates. That is an onerous standard imposed by the two major parties that have a strong interest in excluding any nonparty contend-ers. Most observers would consider 15 percent of the vote a successful result for an Independent *on election day*, over ten times the typical splinter-party tally, yet the politi-cal establishment sets that hurdle even to qualify for the campaign participation needed to produce that level of support, a political catch-22.

Debates are signature events for staking out a candi-date's positions on the issues. As Chapter Two laid out, most policy positions incubated in highly partisan primaries have slender support. A debate setting for showing voters that they have a real choice represents the Independent candidate's biggest breakout opportunity, as Perot's candidacy demonstrated. Having an Independent in the debate would also undermine the Republican National Committee's threat not to participate—who would risk giving two opponents ninety minutes of free national network coverage to lambaste your empty chair? To clear this critical hurdle of debate participation, an Independent must generate a foundation of early momentum.

The sand thus runs out on mounting an effective independent candidacy before and possibly well before the major party candidates are known. (This may have contributed to Mark Cuban's decision not to run in 2020.) Assuming that major party nominees will prove unacceptable and laying the groundwork for an independent candidacy even before the primaries begin is the only way to protect against another nega-lection.

Many voters nevertheless delay their support for an Independent candidacy, fearing the risk of unintended consequences, especially the possibility of damaging the least bad of the two major party candidates. Democrats often cite Ralph Nader's Green Party candidacy in 2000 as a cautionary tale because it may have tipped the razor-thin balance in favor of Bush 43. Howard Schultz cited this as one reason for not running in 2020.

The election timeline largely alleviates these concerns.

Party nominees will be known by midsummer 2024, if not sooner, leaving ample time for an Independent to withdraw from the general election and declare support for a moderate major party nominee. Any Independent entering the race on a centrist platform would hardly risk splitting the vote of a like-minded candidate who enjoyed the inestimable advantage of party backing. It would defeat the goal of the candidacy to no useful purpose. No Labels has already declared its intention not to let a candidate using its ballot line play the spoiler, a belt-and-suspenders safeguard. The feared consequences of a third candidate siphoning off votes appear overblown in 2024.

The greater unknown is whether anyone suitable to serve as president of the United States can be persuaded to run outside of the major parties. That decision requires a long-shot, expensive, life-changing commitment and huge loss of privacy for a high-profile individual who has options far less odious than the grind of a national campaign. This is a tough sell by any measure.

Only one reward can overcome such weighty drawbacks: *a chance to make a difference in America's moment of need.* Clear majorities of voters are profoundly dissatisfied and even fearful over the current state and direction of the union, as they should be. The leaders and most likely candidates of the major parties offer only more of the same or worse. Trump and Biden *boast* of their great accomplishments in office, leaving most voters shaking their heads. What would it take for them to acknowledge failure? China annexing Taiwan? Social Security insolvency? A $2 trillion deficit, or 6 percent unemployment, or 10 percent inflation? All of the above? Or would the inestimable value of remaining in power outweigh even that? When leaders weigh their political and partisan successes more heavily than the nation's worsening problems, change is needed. It must begin at the top because beginning at the bottom would be too slow to address America's looming problems. The millions of Americans seeking a president with a mainstream, pragmatic worldview could be enough to attract the kind of candidate that the nation deserves.

Voters also express the fear that a successful candidate's campaign positions may change in the Oval Office, as occurred with Biden's leftward slide in 2020. The best chance of avoiding this bait and switch is to fix the candidate's basic positions on major issues as early and as firmly as possible, insisting on *commitment*, clear and unequivocal, to moderate/centrist governance if elected, whatever pressures the parties may bring to bear. These commitments could include the following:

Fiscal responsibility: The record-shattering debt accumulation of the last two decades must end. A centrist presidential candidate should commit to declining deficits, using veto threats if needed, with the goal of balancing the budget while in office.

Inflation: Excess monetary and fiscal stimulus as the norm for economic policy must end. The candidate must pledge to appoint Federal Reserve governors who take their duty to protect the dollar seriously, along with the commitment to fiscal austerity until inflation stays below 2 percent annually through a business cycle.

Energy and climate change: Yo-yo policies go nowhere and achieve nothing. The world needs another energy revolution, and the US is the natural leader. A centrist candidate must commit to maintaining American energy sufficiency while sharply expanding R & D investments in carbon-free technologies that are cheap enough to induce China and other developing economies to adopt them.

Immigration and border security: This is an opportunity masquerading as a problem: invite more willing workers to fill available jobs, naturalize the Dreamers, and vigorously exclude the uninvited. Partisans on both sides have proved their preference for keeping immigration as a wedge issue. The next president must commit to breaking this congressional logjam and enacting the comprehensive and balanced reform that is available for the taking.

Global standing: Vacillating leadership has weakened America's influence in the world. A centrist candidate must commit to a bipartisan foreign policy, restoring a domestic consensus and rebuilding the trust of America's allies, while maintaining armed forces more than adequate to protect US interests and preserve the principle of self-determination for all free nations.

Bipartisan governance: A centrist candidate must commit to being president of all the American people, in word and deed. That includes reaching out to both parties and to independent leaders in search of common ground instead of angling for partisan advantage at every turn. Compromise must again become a source of strength, not a sign of weakness.

Civility: The name-calling and demonization on both sides must end, with the next president leading by example. Rudeness has never enhanced a position.

These commitments are illustrative. Other equally important undertakings may be needed. The vital point is that voters willing to consider electing the first independent president since Washington deserve to *know* rather than *guess* what they are voting for.

Who?

The appendix lists some Americans who have been mentioned as possible presidential or vice-presidential candidates in 2024 who could plausibly run as moderates within the major parties or as centrist Independents. They may or may not be interested; the author has no inside information. Only time will tell if voters have much interest in them.

The point of this list is that America remains rich in capable and experienced people who might be worthy of holding such high office. The major parties are at fault for not embracing such candidates. With the nation's fixation on the chaos that has engulfed the White House for too long, they do not receive the attention they deserve. The major parties' extremist wings will spare no effort to keep them out. In 2024, with those fringes in such bad repute, voters might have that once-in-a-lifetime chance to let them in.

CONCLUSION

It's always darkest before the dawn.

—Proverb

Millions of Americans yearn to vote in favor of the best candidate in 2024 rather than against the worst. The pressing challenge facing the nation is to translate this desire into effective action: either a strong enough primary showing by a moderate to win a major party nomination or a general election campaign by a centrist Independent who can attract a critical mass of voters and potentially prevail. These objectives must be pursued in tandem because any effective independent run would have to be in process before the parties nominate their candidates.

This slim volume is merely an overture, an introduction to the formidable task at hand. Whatever the author's pipe dreams, only a relative handful of Americans will ever read this sentence. Mass appeal needs a broad range of short-form, easily digested media, new and old, including videos, podcasts, websites, radio and television news interviews, op-ed pieces, speeches to civic groups—whatever opportunities present themselves to reach persuadable voters. No Labels has made a brave start on the large-scale logistics of this task, but much more will also be needed from other sources, national, state, and local. This book and the ongoing effort to develop its thesis are intended to provide support, structure, and a point of reference for more popular and accessible information streams.

The printed word soon becomes dated in a fast-evolving political climate. The website purplepresidency.org supports this volume with newer information, elaboration, links to useful resources for further study, and a forum for online discussions. Readers with questions or comments should post them there. The website also features updates to report pertinent developments and tie them into this discussion where possible or amend this text when needed, along with links to other like-minded political and voter organizations.

Americans devoted to a return to bipartisanship and decency in Washington have already committed thousands of working hours and millions of dollars to lay a foundation for change, but this is barely a start. Only shaking up the major parties and the presidential election process will justify such an effort. Partisans of left and right will try to keep their grip on elections at any cost. Polls show that the popular support for more mainstream candidates is broad based, but it is not yet close to matching the fringes' intensity and organization. This effort depends on morphing sentiment into evangelism capable of moving the needle in 2024. This will require the best efforts and energy of millions of people.

Sincere and well-meaning naysayers are everywhere, warning the author and other like-minded individuals that this undertaking is hopeless. It is too big. Washington's ways are impervious to mere citizens' wishes. It is a waste of time and energy. On its face, that seems like sensible advice—why would anyone try to accomplish something on this scale against the wishes of powerful Washington interests?—but the founding fathers believed otherwise. They staked their lives and founded a nation on the novel premise that America's government should represent the views and serve the interests of its citizens. With the republic in crisis, there is no better time to test their beliefs, however long the odds may seem.

A tsunami begins as a seismic disturbance producing an indetectable bump in the ocean, its power becoming apparent only as it nears land. Make a difference. Ignore the naysayers. Join the bump.

APPENDIX

Sample list of possible major party moderate or independent centrist candidates

CHARLIE BAKER, R, 66	Former two-term governor of Massachusetts. Consistently high approval ratings in a blue state. Considered fiscally conservative, socially liberal.
MICHAEL BENNET, D, 58	Third-term senator from Colorado. Supports both renewable energy and natural gas development. Periodically supports bipartisan efforts.
MARK CUBAN, I, 64	Entrepreneur, investor, media figure. Self-described socially centric, economically conservative. Has previously expressed interest in a presidential run.

DOUG DUCEY, R, 58	Entrepreneur, investor, former two-term governor of Arizona. Censured by Arizona Republican party for failure to support Trump's efforts to overturn 2020 election results.
NIKKI HALEY, R, 51	Former ambassador to the UN and two-term senator from South Carolina. Mainstream conservative; favors Republican outreach to broader constituency; critic of Trump post-election conduct.
LARRY HOGAN, R, 66	Former two-term governor of Maryland. Governed as a moderate, remaining popular in a blue state. Prominent Republican critic of Trump. National cochair of No Labels.
JOHN KASICH, R, 70	Former two-term governor and four-term House member from Ohio. Prominent Trump critic. Mainstream fiscal conservative. Advocates bipartisan efforts in Congress.

AMY KLOBUCHAR, D, 62	Third-term senator from Minnesota. Presidential candidate in 2020. Generally a mainstream liberal, she has supported multiple bipartisan efforts in the Senate.
JOE MANCHIN, D, 75	Businessman, former two-term governor and current two-term senator from West Virginia. Frequent supporter of bipartisan efforts. Supported Republicans in blocking BBB in 2021.
EVAN MCMULLIN, I, 46	Politician. Quit Republican party in 2016 over Trump nomination. Narrowly lost Utah Senate race in 2022, running as independent in Republican state. Mainstream conservative economically.
WILLIAM MCRAVEN, I, 67	Four-star admiral and special operations commander. Describes his politics as "dead center." David Brooks' column regarding No Labels mentioned him as a potential candidate.

GARY PETERS, D, 64	Second term senator, former three-term House member from Michigan, former investment adviser. Ranked as one of the most bipartisan senators, frequently supports business interests.
ROB PORTMAN, R, 68	Former seven-term House member and two-term senator from Ohio and Office of Management and Budget director in Bush 43 administration. Deficit hawk. Senate leader in bipartisan outreach and critic of partisan gridlock.
HOWARD SCHULTZ, I, 69	Businessman with rags-to-riches story. Considered independent presidential run in 2020, withdrawing over concern it would help reelect Trump. Fiscally conservative, socially moderate to liberal.
KYRSTEN SINEMA, I, 46	First-term senator, former House member from Arizona. Refused to abolish the filibuster, registered as independent and is co-authoring a bipartisan immigration bill. Socially liberal, fiscally moderate.

ACKNOWLEDGMENTS

Writing a book is a solitary endeavor that needs a village behind it. In my village, the wise elders have been Gary Davidson, Tom Harrison, Al Kuenn, Arnie Kuenn, Bill McLeish, and Linda Rita. Brandon Coward at Amplify Publishing has offered excellent guidance and indulged my numerous last-minute changes. Profound thanks for all your support.

ENDNOTES

CHAPTER ONE

1 Bruce Thompson, "How Trump Polarized Voters," *Urban Milwaukee*, July 21, 2021, https://urbanmilwaukee.com/2021/07/21/data-wonk-how-trump-polarized-voters/.

2 Elaine Kamarck, *Primary Politics*, 3rd ed. (Washington, DC: Brookings Institution Press, 2018), 195. See also Jonathan Rauch and Ray La Raja, "Too Much Democracy Is Bad for Democracy," *Atlantic*, December 2019, 62 ("major American parties have ceded unprecedented power to primary voters. It's a radical experiment—and it's failing.").

3 Morris Fiorina, *Disconnect* (Norman: University of Oklahoma Press, 2011), 81.

4 Francis Fukuyama, *Liberalism and Its Discontents* (New York: Farrar, Strauss & Giroux, 2022), chapters 6–7.

5   Jonathan Rauch, "How American Politics Went Insane," *Atlantic*, July/August 2016.

6   A. W. Geiger, "For many voters, it's not which presidential candidate they're for but which they're against," Pew Research Center, September 2, 2016, https://www.pewresearch.org/fact-tank/2016/09/02/for-many-voters-its-not-which-presidential-candidate-theyre-for-but-which-theyre-against/.

7   E.g., "This lawsuit represents a historic and profound abuse of the judicial process."—Judge Linda Parker, Eastern District of Michigan. "This court has been presented with strained legal arguments without merit and speculative accusations . . . unsupported by evidence."—Judge Matthew Brann, Middle District of Pennsylvania.

8   "The Squad" consists of six young, avowedly leftist Democratic members of the House, originally formed following the 2018 election.

9   Dante Chinni, "Poll: Half of Voters Have Already Decided Against Trump in 2020," NBC News, November 3, 2019, https://www.nbcnews.com/politics/meet-the-press/poll-half-voters-have-already-decided-against-trump-2020-n1075746.

10   Biden–Sanders Unity Task Force Recommen-

dations, https://www.documentcloud.org/
documents/6983111-UNITY-TASK-FORCE-REC-
OMMENDATIONS.

11   "The Trump–Biden Presidential Contest," Pew
Research Center, October 9, 2020, https://
www.pewresearch.org/politics/2020/10/09/
the-trump-biden-presidential-contest/.

12   This discussion is largely based on Jonathan
Martin and Alexander Burns, *This Will Not Pass*
(New York: Simon & Schuster, 2022), chapters 9,
10, and 12.

13   Martin and Burns, *This Will Not Pass*, 268–75.

14   "Key Results—October," Harvard CAPS / Harris,
October 4, 2022, https://harvardharrispoll.com/
key-results-october-3/ (slide 4).

15   Compare Brad Dress, "Independents broke for
Democrats by 4 points in midterms," *The Hill*,
November 9, 2022, https://thehill.com/homenews/
campaign/3727958-independents-broke-for-demo-
crats-by-4-points-in-midterms-ap-survey/ to "Behind
Biden's 2020 Victory," Pew Research Center, June
30, 2021, https://www.pewresearch.org/poli-
tics/2021/06/30/behind-bidens-2020-victory/.

16   Trump also opposed moderate Republican senator
Lisa Murkowski in Alaska. His candidate won the

primary, but Murkowski qualified for the general election under Alaska's ranked choice voting, where voters comfortably re-elected her.

17   "Key Results—November," Harvard CAPS / Harris, November 18, 2022, https://harvardharrispoll. com/key-results-november-2/.

18   "Electoral Vote Map," Goddard Media, https://elec-toralvotemap.com/2000-election-results/. Light gray states are Republican wins, dark gray Democratic.

19   Megan Brenan, "Americans Less Optimistic about Next Generation's Future," Gallup, October 25, 2022 https://news.gallup.com/poll/403760/amer-icans-less-optimistic-next-generation-future.aspx, poll date September 2022 (access pdf for complete question responses).

CHAPTER TWO

1   CPI-U, All Urban Consumers, quarterly data, not seasonally adjusted, from the Bureau of Labor Sta-tistics. https://data.bls.gov/cgi-bin/surveymost.

2   "Key results—September," Harvard CAPS / Harris, September 12, 2022, https://harvardharrispoll. com/key-results-september/ (slide 10).

3   Gopi Goda and Evan Soltis, "The Impact of Covid-19 Illnesses on Workers," National Bureau of Economic Research, Working Paper 30435, September 2022, https://www.nber.org/papers/w30435.

4   Debt figures throughout this book are "debt held by the public," i.e., excluding debts that the government owes to itself, available at https://fiscaldata.treasury.gov/datasets/monthly-statement-public-debt/summary-of-treasury-securities-outstanding.

5   Chart based on World Bank Open Data at data.worldbank.org using current US$ GDP figures.

6   Peter G. Peterson Foundation, "Interest Costs on the National Debt Projected to Nearly Triple over the Next Decade," PGPF, July 22, 2021, https://www.pgpf.org/blog/2021/07/interest-costs-on-the-national-debt-projected-to-nearly-triple-over-the-next-decade.

7   "Key Results—October," Harvard CAPS / Harris, Oct. 4, 2022, https://harvardharrispoll.com/key-results-october-3/ (slide 38).

8   California's electricity prices are double those of its neighboring states across the board (residential, commercial, and industrial). U.S. Energy Information Administration, "Electric Sales, Revenue,

and Average Price," EIA, October 6, 2022, Table T4, https://www.eia.gov/electricity/sales_revenue_price/.

9   "Key Results—October," Harvard CAPS / Harris, October 4, 2022, https://harvardharrispoll.com/key-results-october-3/ (slide 39).

10 "Xi Jinping Explains his Political Philosophy," The Scholar's Stage, June 2, 2019, https://scholars-stage.org/xi-jinping-explains-his-political-philosophy/.

11 The date range of 2010–19 excludes the transitory economic impacts of the Great Recession before and the pandemic after. https://www.iea.org/countries.

12 Meng-Tian Huang and Pan-Mao Jai, "Achieving Paris Agreement temperature goals requires carbon neutrality by middle century with far-reaching transitions in the whole society," *Advances in Climate Change Research*, Vol. 12, Issue 2, April 2021, https://www.sciencedirect.com/science/article/pii/S1674927821000435, 281-86.

13 See e.g., Carl Minzner, "China's Doomed Fight against Demographic Decline," *Foreign Affairs*, May 3, 2022, https://www.foreignaffairs.com/articles/china/2022-05-03/

chinas-doomed-fight-against-demographic-de-cline?check_logged_in=1.

14 Michael Standaert, "Despite Pledges to Cut Emissions, China Goes on a Coal Spree," YaleEnvironment360, March 24, 2021, https://e360.yale.edu/features/despite-pledges-to-cut-emissions-china-goes-on-a-coal-spree.

15 "It is not a secret that COP26 is a failure." Greta Thunberg, "COP26: Greta Thunberg tells protest that COP26 has been a 'failure'," BBC, November 5, 2021, https://www.bbc.com/news/uk-scot-land-glasgow-west-59165781; Thunberg skipped COP27 altogether, commenting that "the COPS are not really working." "Greta Thunberg to skip 'greenwashing' Cop27 climate summit in Egypt," *Guardian*, Oct. 30, 2022, https://www.theguardian.com/environment/2022/oct/31/greta-thunberg-to-skip-greenwashing-cop27-cli-mate-summit-in-egypt.

16 "United in Science: We are Heading in the Wrong Direction," United Nations Climate Change, September 13, 2022, https://unfccc.int/news/united-in-science-we-are-heading-in-the-wrong-direction.

17 Maxime Babics, et al., "Unleashing the Full Power of Perovskite/Silicon Tandem Modules with Solar

Trackers," *ACS Energy Letters*, April 6, 2022, https://pubs.acs.org/doi/10.1021/acsenergy-lett.2c00442. Describes the impending gains from these advances for the technically inclined. These technologies could finally fulfill the promise of scalable, truly cheap renewable power.

18 Katherine Gehl and Michael Porter, *The Politics Industry* (Boston: Harvard Business Review Press, 2020), 73–75.

19 Stuart Anderson, "A Review of Trump Immigration Policy," *Forbes*, August 26, 2020, https://www.forbes.com/sites/stuartanderson/2020/08/26/fact-check-and-review-of-trump-immigration-policy/?sh=6d39dfa256c0.

20 "Could Immigration Solve the US Worker Shortage?" Goldman Sachs, May 31, 2022, https://www.goldmansachs.com/insights/pages/could-immigration-solve-the-us-worker-shortage.html.

21 "Donald Trump Job Approval: Handling of Immigration and Border Security," University of Texas at Austin, June 2019, https://texaspolitics.utexas.edu/set/donald-trump-job-approval-handling-immigration-and-border-security-june-2019#ideology.

22 Refugees and Asylum, U.S. Citizenship and Immigration Services, https://www.uscis.gov/

humanitarian/refugees-asylum.

23   Eileen Sullivan, "Biden Administration Has Admit-
      ted One Million Migrants to Await Hearings,"
      New York Times, September 6, 2022, https://
      www.nytimes.com/2022/09/06/us/politics/asy-
      lum-biden-administration.html.

24   Alicia Caldwell, "Migrant Surge Overwhelms El
      Paso," *Wall Street Journal*, December 16, 2022, A3.

25   "On immigration, most buying into the idea of
      'invasion' at southern border," Ipsos, August 18,
      2022, https://www.ipsos.com/en-us/news-polls/
      npr-immigration-perceptions-august-2022.

26   Andrew Arthur, "Polling Shows Trouble for Biden
      and strong support for border security among
      Texas Hispanics," Center for Immigration Studies,
      April 18, 2022, https://cis.org/Arthur/Polling-
      Shows-Trouble-Biden; "Key results—September,"
      Harvard CAPS / Harris, September 12, 2022,
      https://harvardharrispoll.com/key-results-sep-
      tember/ (slide 10).

27   See e.g., David Schleifer and Will Friedman,
      "Where Americans Stand on Immigration," Public
      Agenda, August 2020, https://www.publicagenda.
      org/reports/where-americans-stand-on-immigra-
      tion-a-hidden-common-ground-report/.

28   Stephen Kalin, "Xi's Saudi Visit Reflects China's Rise in Mideast," *Wall Street Journal*, December 8, 2022, A13.

29   Hal Brands and Michael Beckley, *Danger Zone* (New York: W. W. Norton, 2022), especially chapters 2 ("Peak China") and 4.

30   "Key results—September," Harvard CAPS / Harris, September 12, 2022, https://harvardharrispoll. com/key-results-september/ (slide 15).

31   Jill Mislinski, "Median Household Incomes by Age Bracket: 1967–2020," VettaFi Advisor Perspectives, October 26, 2021, https://www.advisorperspectives. com/dshort/updates/2021/10/26/median-house-hold-incomes-by-age-bracket-1967-2020.

32   See, for example, Congressional Research Service, "Poverty Among the Population Aged 65 and Over," April 14, 2021, crs.congress.gov, report #R45791.

33   Social Security's history of expansions is described in John Cogan, *The High Cost of Good Intentions* (Stanford University Press, 2017), chapters 8, 10, 11, and 13.

34   Social Security's 2022 OASDI Trustees' Report at heading IV.A.1. All figures in the text are the trustees' intermediate estimates. https://www.ssa.gov/OACT/TR/2022/.

35   This perverse incentive dates back to Social Securi-
      ty's Depression-era origins: turf out the oldsters so
      younger men could support their families. https://
      www.retiredbrains.com/working-and-benefits.
      html.

36   Michael Sasso and Alexandre Tanzi, "The 'Great
      Retirement' Disconnect that Puzzles U.S. Economists,"
      Bloomberg, March 23, 2022, https://www.bloomberg.
      com/news/articles/2022-03-23/the-great-retirement-
      disconnect-that-puzzles-u-s-economists.

37   Michael Shear, "Obama Pledges Reform of Social
      Security, Medicare Programs," *Washington Post,*
      January 16, 2009, http://www.washington-
      post.com/wp-dyn/content/article/2009/01/15/
      AR2009011504114.html. Obama expressed com-
      plete confidence in his ability to fix the program's
      deepening problems. "Social Security we can solve."
      "Yes we can" remained the mantra. With Social
      Security, maybe he could have if he had tried.

38   Chain-weighted consumer price index assumes
      that consumers substitute away from products that
      become more expensive, e.g., buying plums instead
      of peaches if peaches rise in price.

39   New York Crime Rates: 1960–2019, https://www.
      disastercenter.com/crime/nycrime.htm.

40   Patrick Sharkey, *Uneasy Peace* (New York: W. W. Norton, 2018), 112.

41   Franklin Zimring, *The Great American Crime Decline* (Oxford University Press, 2007), 143. Chapter 6 analyzes New York City's post-COPS crime reduction successes.

42   Chris Smith, "The Controversial Crime-Fighting Program That Changed Big City Policing Forever," *New York Magazine–Intelligencer*, May 2018, https://nymag.com/intelligencer/2018/03/the-crime-fighting-program-that-changed-new-york-forever.html.

43   Data in this paragraph are compiled in Hope Corman and Naci Mocan, "Carrots, Sticks, and Broken Windows," NBER Working Paper 9061, National Bureau of Economic Research, July 2002, at www.nber.org/papers/w9061.

44   Brian McCrone, "Why are Homicides in Philadelphia Near an All-time High?", NBC Philadelphia, November 26, 2020, https://www.nbcphiladelphia.com/news/local/why-are-homicides-in-philadelphia-near-an-all-time-high-here-are-some-factors/2611207/.

45   "Americans' Experiences, Concerns, and Views Related to Gun Violence," AP NORC,

August 23, 2022, https://apnorc.org/projects/americans-experiences-concerns-and-views-related-to-gun-violence/.

46   See Robert Boatright, *Getting Primaried* (Ann Arbor: University of Michigan Press, 2022).

47   Josh Kraushaar, "Democratic meddling pays off," *Axios,* September 18, 2022, https://www.axios.com/2022/09/18/democratic-meddling-results-republican-primaries; Ellen Ioanes, "How a surprising Democratic strategy may have staved off the midterm red wave," *Vox,* November 12, 2022, https://www.vox.com/2022/11/12/23454725/democrat-republican-maga-strategy-midterm-red-wave; Bill Chappell, "Democrats' strategy of boosting far-right candidates seems to have worked," NPR, November 11, 2022, https://www.npr.org/2022/11/11/1135878576/the-democrats-strategy-of-boosting-far-right-candidates-seems-to-have-worked.

48   Joseph Gedeon, "Dem super PAC goes after Republican ahead of N.H. Senate primary," *Politico,* September 2, 2022, https://www.politico.com/news/2022/09/02/dem-super-pac-republican-new-hampshire-senate-primary-00054690; Andrew Dorn and Robert Sherman, "Dems spent

millions backing GOP candidates—will it back-fire?" News Nation, November 3, 2022, https://www.newsnationnow.com/politics/elections-2022/dems-spent-millions-backing-gop-candidates-will-it-backfire/.

49   Gary Jacobson, *A Divider, Not a Uniter,* 2nd ed. (New York: Longman, 2011), 1.

50   "In steady, quiet tones, the vice president-elect laid out a shockingly divisive political agenda for the new Bush administration. . . . He said that the campaign was over and that our actions in office would not be dictated by the things that had to be said in the campaign." Lincoln Chafee, *Against the Tide* (New York: Thomas Dunne Books, 2008), 6–9.

51   Matthew Dickinson, "Some Thoughts on the Stimulus Bill," Presidential Power, February 14, 2009, https://sites.middlebury.edu/presidentialpower/2009/02/14/some-thoughts-on-the-stimulus-bill/. ("Obama lost his first and best opportunity to fulfill his campaign promise to change the tone of Washington politics. . . . The simple fact is his legislative strategy in Congress proved every bit as polarizing as Bush's.")

52   Francois de Soyres, et al., "Fiscal policy and excess inflation during Covid-19," Board of Governors of

the Federal Reserve System, July 15, 2022, https://www.federalreserve.gov/econres/notes/feds-notes/fiscal-policy-and-excess-inflation-during-covid-19-a-cross-country-view-20220715.html.

53   Fukuyama, *Liberalism and Its Discontents*, 154.

CHAPTER THREE

1   Kyrsten Sinema, "Why I'm registering as an independent," *azcentral*, December 9, 2022, https://www.azcentral.com/story/opinion/op-ed/2022/12/09/sen-kyrsten-sinema-of-arizona-why-im-registering-as-an-independent/69712395007/.

2   "Key results—September," Harvard CAPS / Harris, September 12, 2022, https://harvardharrispoll.com/key-results-september/, slide 26. An October 2022 PRRI poll corroborates this result: 42 percent of all Americans, including 57 percent of independents, would vote for a candidate from a third party ideologically situated between the Republican and Democrat parties. https://www.prri.org/research/challenges-in-moving-toward-a-more-inclusive-democracy-findings-from-the-2022-american-values-survey/. In a three-candidate race, 42 percent wins comfortably.

3   On the Perot candidacy generally and its influence in Washington, see Ronald Rapoport and Walter Stone, *Three's a Crowd* (Ann Arbor: University of Michigan Press, 2005).

4   "As partisan antipathy grows, signs of frustration with the two-party system," Pew Research Center, Aug. 9, 2022, https://www.pewresearch.org/politics/2022/08/09/rising-partisan-antipathy-widening-party-gap-in-presidential-job-approval/.

5   "What Does No Labels Stand For," No Labels, https://www.nolabels.org/what-does-no-labels-stand-for.

INDEX

THE PURPLE PRESIDENCY 2024

X

Xi Jinping, 24, 74, 75, 97, 99

Y

Yeats, William Butler, 1
Yellen, Janet, 56

Z

Zelenskyy, Volodymyr, 95
Zimring, Franklin, 116

ABOUT THE AUTHOR

C. Owen Paepke is the author of *The Evolution of Progress* (named best nonfiction book of 1993 by NPR's *Talk of the Nation*) and the three-volume series *The Seinfeld Election*, which was praised by reviewers as "a provocative investigation into the American political divide."

He has spoken and written widely on technology and science policy, including a keynote address on the future of science to the fiftieth anniversary meeting of the Federation of American Scientists and a speech on the prospects for technological and economic progress at the Smithsonian Institution.

He lives in Arizona, where he practiced for many years as an attorney specializing in antitrust and intellectual property, and is a graduate of Stanford and the University of Chicago.